Lockdown Laughs

The Bathroom Book

Gerda Gordon

RINGWOOD PUBLISHING
GLASGOW

First published in Great Britain in 2020

by

Ringwood Publishing, Glasgow.

www.ringwoodpublishing.com

mail@ringwoodpublishing.com

ISBN 978-1-901514-79-7

British Library Cataloguing-in-Publication Data

A catalogue record for this book is available from the British Library

Printed and bound in the UK

by

Lonsdale Direct Solutions

DEDICATION

This book is dedicated to Alex, my husband, aka the dweeb. Thank you for all of your help, encouragement and support.

FOREWORD

On March 23, the United Kingdom was faced with an unprecedented challenge: Lockdown. No pubs, no restaurants, no concerts, no house parties, no visits to or from close friends and loved ones; almost total restriction with no imminent end to the nightmare in sight at the time of publication.

Lockdown has adversely affected every one of us, imposing new levels of stress, anxiety and fear. But alongside all this pain and misery, there has been an impressive reassertion of positive human values and the capacity for resilience.

Moving demonstrations of massive public support for NHS staff and other key front line workers. Communal efforts to organise social and physical support for vulnerable neighbours and groups. One small part of this human capacity to remain positive and find the strength to overcome adversity, has been efforts to find and extract humour from these dire times.

Lockdown Laughs - The Bathroom Book is one such attempt. It began life as Gerda Gordon's one-off attempt to provide a brief smile to her Facebook friends. It was the snowball going down the hill that created an avalanche. It very quickly attracted a growing band of supporters. It became clear Gerda's pals were beginning to look forward to these daily posts as a welcome humorous antidote to the frustrations of lockdown life. For me, it was my go to place every morning I opened my phone to see what mayhem had besieged Gerda and her dweeb the night before!

As weeks turned into months and the number of daily adventures escalated from tens to hundreds, the readership and appreciation of these hilarious reports grew and grew. One of the readers who became a fan was Sandy Jamieson, Chief Executive of Ringwood Publishing. He believed these daily doses of lockdown laughs deserved a wider audience, and that bringing them together into a book was the obvious solution. Hence the emergence of this current volume of Lockdown Laughs.

Several points need to be made about this book. It is NOT meant to be read in serious doses, but rather should be dipped into for light relief when restrictions seem overwhelming. Lockdown Laughs unfailingly offers a laughter antidote across the whole range from bellylaughs, through giggles and sniggers, to grins and smiles.

Lockdown Laughs - the Bathroom Book seeks to offer a temporary escape and comical relief through uproarious lockdown stories. These detail the day-to-day struggles of Gerda and her beloved dweeb Alex, as they strive to maintain an increasingly tenuous hold on their sanity during the ever-increasing pressures of life under lockdown restrictions. With cartoon violence worthy of Tom and Jerry and earth-shattering events on a daily basis rivalling the Simpsons, Gerda and the dweeb live with lockdown 24/7 with every day the exactly the same and every day hilariously different.

Because of this, the book belongs not in the bookcase but in the bathroom or on a coffee table where it can be accessed only one story at a time. With each visit to the loo, and each new story, you can be assured someone had it worse than you during lockdown. After all, how many of us can say we got stuck overnight in the refuse bin, or were chased out of town by a pack of bun-throwing bloodthirsty grannies?

Sympathise with the desperate wife driven to regular Prosecco overdoses and cartoon violence by the dopey daftness of her unintentionally irritating dweeb. And sympathise, equally, with the devoted dweeb as all his attempts to please his 'little cupcake' turn hysterically - and often painfully - wrong. Fair play for Gerda keeping it up, giving us a laugh and gathering such a big readership.

Gerda welcomed the posts being turned into a book, but was insistent from the start that her share of any revenue raised be given to selected charities. Ringwood Publishing was happy to make the same commitment, so readers can be assured that all proceeds from the sale of the book will go the four selected charities - Alzheimer's Scotland, Cancer Research, Children In Need and the Cystic Fibrosis Trust.

So enjoy this book, in the spirit it was written, and help great charities benefit.

Anna Smith, crime writer and journalist

LOCKDOWN, day 1

Monday, March 23, 2020

Today, I awake to confront something the government is insisting on calling lockdown. I'm not sure what it will fully entail, but one thing seems frighteningly clear and that is I will be forced to spend more time in the dire company of someone who laughably calls himself my husband.

I call him the dweeb, or the halfwit, or the dingbat, or a number of other colourful monikers, none of which is complimentary.

It seems a plague called Covid-19 is threatening to wipe out the universe. The situation is serious enough for the powers-that-be to restrict the movements of entire populations throughout the globe.

None of the world's top scientists and eggheads appear to have a clue what is going on. No-one can tell us when the restrictions will be lifted. I am under house arrest in the company of the drongo (another of his little sobriquets). This could be a life sentence, dear friends and fellow-sympathisers. Oh, joy.

Some things never change, though. As I attempt to get out of the scratcher, there is no sign of the person who shares the marital bed. To be fair, he is normally up well before me and, as you will discover in the forthcoming weeks (months? Dear God, years?) he is an early-riser (oh, for goodness sake, you lot at the back, we don't need any sniggering. This is serious).

As is my daily task, I step over his discarded pyjamas. I note these are his favourite Lady Gaga night apparel (don't ask). He is very fastidious about his night-time attire and insists on a change every evening. He visited a 24-Hour Pyjama Shop that was closing down recently and bought about a year's supply. A win-win situation for me for rather than subject me to copious amounts of laundering the dweeb has decided to toss each pair of pyjamas into the bin – or, more accurately, the bedroom floor - after a single night's wear.

Oh, please forgive my rudeness, I haven't introduced myself. My name is Gerda (my mother was German) and the other quarter's name is…actually, dear friends, it is has slipped my mind for the moment. We'll just continue to call him dweeb.

We live in a 240-year-old cottage in a small village on the outskirts of dear old Glasgow. The local worthies are quite an assortment. I'll introduce you to them as we go along. You may find some of them just a tad quirky. Others you may believe should be placed in a rubber padded room for some considerable time.

Over the next few days, you may get the notion I over-indulge in alcohol. I don't have a drink problem, folks. 'I drink. I fall over. No problem.' (copyright: Tommy Cooper esq). I readily admit I do enjoy a glass or two of Prosecco with my breakfast. Well, actually, that's all I have, to be honest. Sometimes a glass manifests into a bottle. Okay, I have been known to get on the outside of a bottle or two of bubbles. I need a good fortification – I said fortification, Edina – most mornings.

Please do not rush to judge, good people. I invite you to spend time with me and observe what I have to tolerate from the dullard on a daily basis and then tell me what you think. For instance, just the other day I asked the little halfwit to sort the washing, separating the colours from the whites. Once he had spent about an hour on a task any self-respecting five year old would unravel in three minutes, I put on a non fast coloured wash and allowed him to sit in front of the machine.

I wondered how long it would take before he exclaimed: 'This is one of my favourite Humphrey Bogart movies.' He took three minutes, dear friends.

This afternoon, for a laugh, the feeble-minded wretch is being sent to the village store (30 seconds away for most people) as I have asked him to buy a tin of peas. Don't worry. I will make sure he is wearing disposable gloves. They will be joined by string so that he doesn't lose them. The money for the peas will be in the gloves.

I know he will be gone for hours. The lollipop lady, Isobel, will be at home during lockdown and I am guessing that social distancing will mean that no-one will assist him in his venture across the road. Inevitably, he will have forgotten about the reason for his mission. The last time I entrusted him with a shopping expedition, I asked him to pick up a newspaper. He came back with a loaf and a steak pie.

Who needs peas, anyway?

Okay, that may have set the scene for what follows. Let's see how this lockdown business plays out, dear friends.

LOCKDOWN, day 10

Wednesday, April 1

Today, I awake and wish fervently that the last nine days have just been one huge, protracted, April Fool's joke. Alas, dear friends and fellow-sympathisers, it's as real as the nose on Gerard Depardieu's face. (What do you mean you always thought that was a dollop of plasticine?)

I sweep my legs out of the marital bed – there is no sign of the dweeb, so that at least is a plus - and I make sure I do not step on his discarded Elton John pyjamas (don't ask).

I head for the fridge and I notice I am running dangerously low on Prosecco. Only two bottles left and, as if by magic, that number is reduced to zilch inside five minutes. This means an emergency pit-stop at the supermarket to stock up is an urgent requirement. First Minister Nicola Sturgeon has ordered inmates only to leave home to buy 'essentials' and I'm sure my friends would agree that covers bubbles. It does in this household, anyway. Other folk can help themselves to milk, butter and bread; I'm heading straight for the wine aisle. It would be a brave or foolish member of Asda who got between me and my quest for suds.

Initially, when I break the news to the dork that we are off to the shops, he throws the anticipated tantrum, but the promise of an Easter egg (they'll be half-price or less) consoles him. I might even pick up some hot cross buns for good measure. If the husband behaves, I promise him a hurl in the trolley.

You should see his wee face. It doesn't take much to keep him happy. When we get home, I will be dispatching the pillock to the garden to feed the birds. I will also pick up a box of suet balls. The box says it contains 150. A neighbour once told me that he no longer buys the product as he once counted them and there were only 149; yes, I do know some strange people. The husband's task will be to count said suet balls. He will be outdoors for ages.

Once he has used his fingers and thumbs to start the count, he will struggle to undo the Velcro on his shoes so he can continue to count using his toes. By this stage, of course, he will have long forgotten which number he has reached. Naturally, determined to see the task through to its conclusion, he will begin again.

As it happens, folks, he counted 130 suet balls, but, in all honesty, I think he might have eaten a few while I was replenishing my Prosecco paradise and was not paying close enough attention.

The unfortunate chap was up all night. I almost felt sorry for him. I said almost.

LOCKDOWN, day 24

Wednesday, April 15

Today, I am to keep the dweeb busy. I am going to send him out to wash the wheely bins.

This is my main aim for the day – and sampling a few jolts of Prosecco, too, of course – as I venture out of the marital bed while sidestepping his discarded Bruce Forsyth pyjamas (don't ask) and head for my first embrace of the fridge. Fortified – I said fortified, you lot at the back – I am ready for another day shut away from civilisation with the halfwit who has blighted my life.

His Speedos are looked out. His water wings are still kicking about from the practice egg hunt. I have found his flippers and snorkel. I will connect the water hose to the tap, turn it on and send him outdoors yet again.

I shall be watching from a safe distance: we don't want any harm to come to the wee soul, (chance would be a fine thing) and, naturally (considering there is a 'y' in the day), I will have a medicinal glass of Prosecco to hand.

I wonder how long it will be before he is face down inspecting the bottom of the wheely bin, legs akimbo, screaming for help. It can't be worse than Monday evening when I put him on gutter-cleaning duties. Yes, I was aware this included a ladder, but for his protection, I encased him in bubble wrap.

It goes without saying he fell off the roof. The neighbours thought we were under a machine-gun attack from some sort of terrorist cell. He didn't help the situation when he attempted to stand up and toppled over again, sending out what sounded like a second salvo of gunfire.

The neighbourhood went into double lockdown. I didn't think it was possible. A swarm of armed police and several helicopters descended on the village just to discover a poor soul festooned in bubble wrap finding great difficulty in remaining upright.

They charged him with being a public nuisance. I could have told them that decades ago.

LOCKDOWN, day 30

Tuesday, April 21

Today, I am going to give the dweeb a bit of time off chores as he has been slightly traumatised over the last few days.

Now completely free of bubble wrap and having satisfied MI5 with his explanation for sending our village into a full-blown panic (all charges have been dropped, rejoice), I have asked him to feed the ducks at a nearby pond.

The poor soul hasn't had much exercise recently, what with all that toppling over, rolling around and creating mayhem with intermittent bubble wrap explosions audible for miles, and I reckon he is entitled to stretch his legs.

I notice he has been walking in a curious fashion recently and I have put that down to lack of exercise. Though perhaps it has something to do with that missing snorkel he was playing with several nights ago which we still haven't located.

I inform him that, with Ms Sturgeon's allowance of one hour of exercise a day, he has accumulated twenty-six hours' worth of freedom. In theory, he could be out of my hair for some considerable amount of time, though I've more chance of a Lotto win. He has bread to feed the ducks, but I am guessing he will get a tad confused - and famished - with all that walking and eat it himself before he gets anywhere near the pond.

Alas, this has happened in the past. Once, he returned and I asked him if the ducks had enjoyed their lunch. He muttered 'Of course", but I noticed the tell-tale crumbs around his chops. I didn't tell him he had been rumbled. Also, I thought it quite advisable to say nothing since the bread was about two weeks out of date.

The poor chap was up most of the night. Not possessing the digestive system of our feathered aquatic friends, some of the noises from the loo were quite melodic.

Today, though, he is well-attired: waders, tee shirt and his favourite pink fluorescent thong. (I wouldn't want him improperly turned out should he be struck by a passing bus, train, truck or cyclist.)

I only had room to sew his initials into the thong, but hope that's enough to aid the police should they have to escort him home. . . .

Again, I am waving to him now, dear friends, as his pasty cheeks waddle down the sidewalk. Here's to several dolt-free hours to myself. I'll open a bottle and drink to that.

LOCKDOWN, day 35

Sunday, April 26

Today, I arouse myself (oh, for goodness sake, you lot at the back) and find no sign of the dweeb who shares the marital bed. I step over his discarded Mel Gibson pyjamas (don't ask) and arrive at the front room via the kitchen where I quench my thirst with a bottle of refreshing Prosecco.

I discover the dingbat wearing his Sunday best and clutching his cherished tambourine. He usually goes to church and plays along (out of time) to the hymns. If he has been particularly good during the week and has not overly irritated me, I let him take his triangle as well.

You should have seen his wee face when I had to break the news that Sunday services had been cancelled for the foreseeable.

In any case, he seems to have forgotten that he has been barred from our local church. At the Christmas Carol concert, the minister took exception to him changing the chorus in 'Oh Come All Ye Faithful' to that from 'Honky Tonk Woman' while gyrating much in the fashion of a deranged Mick Jagger. I confess we'd both imbibed some quantity of alcohol beforehand.

Who would have thought our vicar, no spring chicken, could have moved so swiftly while administering smelling salts to at least eight of his swooning flock in a breathtaking sequence?

It is hoped Mrs Gilhooley, a well-respected parishioner of the community, is allowed out of her trauma centre some time soon.

However, out of the goodness of my heart, I might let him out into the garden when the church bells ring at 11am.

I will love it when he says: 'I didn't know they would sound the bells during the lockdown.' And I will reply: 'What bells? I hear no bells.' Then I will pour myself a large Prosecco while he wanders around the garden, lost in thought.

It should keep him occupied for a few hours. Happy days, dear friends.

LOCKDOWN, day 39

Thursday, April 30

How excited is the dweeb who masquerades as the husband? The enthusiastic chap is up with the lark this morning bouncing with expectancy, like a kid on Christmas Day.

At first, I thought it was all down to last night's curry.

I have told him that he can stay up until 8pm to applaud the NHS and, because it is a special occasion, I will consent to his request of being allowed to take his tambourine into the street. I will remind him it is not compulsory to have his mouth open while he shakes the instrument.

The well-meaning wee soul has also been informed he can join in Captain Tom Moore's 100th Birthday celebrations.

He has vigorously polished his shoes and looked out his kilt. Judging by the reflection in his gleaming footwear, the doofus has forgotten his undercrackers.

I have rummaged through his sporran - an action which actually brought something akin to a smile to his wee face - but, sadly, there is no money to be found. Alas, it looks as though I'll have to dip into my savings to buy extra injections of Prosecco.

I spent yesterday afternoon teaching him the words to the time-honoured ditty 'Happy Birthday' though I fear he'll have forgotten them by 8:05pm. That being the case, I will etch them on the back of his hand. I don't want the neighbours thinking he is a touch slow on the uptake (as if they did not figure this out years ago after the infamous Road-Sweeping Incident, but that's a story for another day. Suffice to say, it didn't end well.)

He will be out in the front garden, his mouth organ set up a la Bob Dylan when he gave it pelters during 'The Answer My Friend Is Blowing

In The Wind'. By the way, I'm reliably informed Dylan wrote this song as a reply to the oft-asked question: How many beans are there in a tin of Heinz? I acknowledge that snippet of information may not be 100 per cent accurate.

I digress. With the harmonica in harness, that will free his hands to play the bagpipes before the poor soul, gasping and out of puff after a minute or so, moves onto the tambourine.

I will pay particular attention to him regarding the bagpipes. I doubt if the neighbourhood has forgotten the incident with Mrs Brown's cocker spaniel when the husband attempted to pipe in the New Year. It took him about ten minutes to figure out why he could not get a tune out of Fido.

Apparently, Fido, normally such an affectionate pooch, refused to leave a dark location behind a wardrobe for about a week after the episode.

Wish me luck, dear friends. This could be a long night. I will keep you up to speed tomorrow when, hopefully, I will be here to recant the happenings of the big event.

Lashings of Prosecco may help me through.

LOCKDOWN, day 50

Monday, May 11

What to do today with the dweeb who masquerades as a husband?

The poor soul feels he needs to contribute something in these testing times. I haven't the heart to tell him to stay in bed.

I was thinking that we could have some fun with the cyclists who have invaded the village in their thousands since lockdown. It's like living in the Champs-Elysees with the Tour de France in full swing.

The husband, armed with his peashooter, can aim at them from the windows upstairs (generally, we only open these windows to applaud our wonderful NHS workers). Don't worry, I have superglued his shorts to the wall to make absolutely certain he doesn't topple out.

That would be more than alarming. I mean to say, my prized rose bush is directly under the window and I don't want him bleeding all over the flowers. He would make such a frightful mess, wouldn't he?

I admit, though, it would make an interesting insurance claim.

You may think me callous to set my husband on those pesky cyclists, but I assure you they are safe enough. Apart from the fact that they are wearing helmets, by the time the husband has managed to load his peashooter - for goodness sake you lot at the back stop sniggering, - they will probably be in another country.

Plus there is the small matter of the unfortunate chap never mastering the complexities of a peashooter.

One of these days I will get around to advising him the instrument works best when you blow and not suck.

I like to keep him busy. The other day, one of my four adorable sisters - I knew they would come in handy some day - came up with the bright idea that he might have fun painting rainbows for the NHS. What could possibly go wrong?

When we participated in the 'Bears At The Front Window' innovation for the NHS, the husband mistook bear for bare. The neighbours still haven't recovered.

He stood there in his birthday suit for the best part of six hours and still is unaware of his faux pas. Poor soul, on the rare occasion he is allowed out, neighbours point and laugh. I haven't the heart to tell him why. Ignorance is bliss, after all. Anyway, I digress. Back to the rainbow paintings. The dweeb has donned his raincoat and wellies. Maybe, some time in the future, I will allow him to purchase a beret a la Rembrandt, Van Gogh etc.

At the moment, however, he will have to make do with a shower cap.

I expect the exercise will end in tears. The house will likely resemble an explosion in a paintworks. I also fear he will get a tad confused and attempt to consume litres of paint, thinking them different coloured pots of frosting or jello. I will do my best to keep an eye on the poor sap, though the bottom of a Prosecco bottle often blocks my vision. We are, by now, on first-name basis with the staff at the local A&E.

As if the NHS doesn't have enough to deal with already. Wish us luck, dear friends.

LOCKDOWN, day 52

Wednesday, May 13

Today, the dweeb aka the husband informs me that he wants to do some DIY. (Gawd help me.)

Now, from the outset, I have to inform you DIY means Destroy It Yourself to my other half. I recall one evening a few years ago, when he decided to put a nail in the wall.

The village was without electricity for the entire weekend.

Let loose, the husband possesses the capabilities to wreak more havoc than a Hydrogen bomb.

Anyway, on this occasion, he tells me he would like to try again - put a nail in the wall, not plunge the neighbourhood into darkened turmoil -and admits it is just a few prints and a small brass plaque.

Believing the world cannot have any more bad news visited upon it, I have relented and I even looked out his Bob The Builder outfit which, naturally, comes complete with an all-important hard hat.

He is allowed the use of my oven gloves so his thumbs have some protective padding when he inevitably bashes them continually with the hammer. He has never quite mastered the art of hitting the nail on the head, much preferring to take the thumb route. On occasion, he varies his approach and sets about trying to flatten a hitherto perfect index finger.

Yes, dear friends and fellow-sympathisers, you're quite right, we don't require a loyalty card for the local A&E.

The plaque is going above the door in what he terms his study/ dungeon. (If only.) I am guessing that it will remain in situ, balancing delicately until the acid test of actually closing the door.

He could become the first man in history to slice off his toes while placing a nail in the wall.

16

If I ever allowed him the use of a saw, he would probably take down a small country.

Getting back to his random assaults on the village's voltage, I am now insisting he performs such feats while standing bare-footed in a bucket of water.

That'll teach him.

Prosecco in hand (purely for medicinal purposes, you understand), I will be standing well back.

LOCKDOWN, day 55

Saturday, May 20

Today, the dweeb wants to prepare the steaks. (Jeezo, is there no end to this misery?)

One look at his wee face and how could I turn him down?

I look out his Fireman Sam outfit so that he looks the part when the local fire fighters turn up.

Naturally, the fire extinguisher is where I can get at it in double-quick time.

The poor soul is living under the mistaken belief he is quite handy in the kitchen. He reckons it is his weekend duty to raid the freezer for a couple of slabs of meat. To be fair, this is a manoeuvre he has perfected over the years.

Naturally, I follow him to return the pizzas, fish, chicken and, of course, ice cream back to where they belong. He hasn't quite mastered that skill yet, but we live in hope. He's a sort of single-minded kind of bloke. Multi-tasking is not for him and he is still working on walking and whistling at the same time.

Anyway, once he has liberated the steaks, he will then go and fetch a hammer from the garden shed. He once witnessed a TV chef tenderise a steak by gently tapping it with a small mallet. Of course, the husband's approach to preparing the food isn't quite aligned with that of Gordon Ramsay and Co.

He pulverises the steak until it is about a centimetre thick and has taken on the dimensions of a manhole cover.

And then he looks out his trusty turbo-charged flamethrower. I've begged him to grill or cook the steaks like normal people do, but he stubbornly believes his method is the best.

While I settle down at six o'clock, I will detect some crazy whirring sounds from the kitchen, flames shooting out from under the door, interlaced with some inevitable cursing, and two minutes later I will receive my scorched dinner.

Well done? More a case of incinerated.

Later on, to fight off the hunger pangs, I'll have an emergency sandwich when he is not looking.

Washed down, of course, with the mandatory glass or three of Prosecco.

LOCKDOWN, day 58

Tuesday, May 19

Today, the husband and I are off to the supermarket for 'essentials' – the supply of Prosecco has inexplicably evaporated. It's quite amazing how quickly twenty bottles of the stuff can vanish into the ether, isn't it?

The fridge and freezer are also bereft of lumpy stuff (aka blotting paper) and there are only so many packets of crisps you can eat in one day.

However, to deflect him from the anticipated tantrum, I have told him we are off to a disco. He'll never know the difference.

Just to ensure my slight act of deception goes undetected by the poor soul, I will allow him to wear his headband, so favoured by Dire Straits' Mark Knopfler.

You should see the husband on air guitar. It is quite an experience. He's got all the moves. That Pete Townshend has got a lot to answer for, I can tell you. It's worth it, though, when you see how thrilled he is when I buy him a new one every Christmas.

His chunky leg-warmers are likely to come out of the mothballs, too. He looks like a yeti who has had an argument with a razor from the knees up.

It may also be a day for an outing for his favourite leopard-skin thong. Donning it never fails to bring a smile to his face. It's the little things in life - and, alas, little is the operative word - that keep him happy.

Anyway, we will reach the supermarket where we will be asked to queue and bouncers on the door will randomly allow people in to the premises. He'll probably think he is at Studio 54.

Once inside, there will be insufferable music - something from the Wurzels, the Archies or Chas and Dave - and the dork will automatically reach for his air guitar - strapped to his back for safekeeping - and go through the full routine. He will sing along loudly (out of tune, of course) and, people will point and laugh.

Meanwhile, I will frantically stock up with Prosecco.

And, if there is any space left in the trolley, I'll maybe chuck in a couple packets of crisps.

LOCKDOWN, day 61

Friday, May 22

Today, the weather is not too great so I am tinkering with the notion of teaching the dweeb the fine art of ironing.

Naturally, I will be doing this with some trepidation.

All we need is for the phone to ring, he'll get confused and lift the sizzling iron to his ear.

The scorch marks on his face would take some explaining to the neighbours, I suppose.

However, his Speedos do need pressed and, given my delicate nature, I would much prefer not to be asked to handle them. I don't really even want to be in the same room as those items, if I am being honest.

However, I believe a nice, crisp crease will perhaps make him look a bit more presentable. Well, presentable to someone who needs a guide dog to help them get around.

I must also make sure that he is not wearing them at the time. When it comes to the dolt, dear friends, you can't take anything for granted.

In fact, a couple of years ago, he did create a little damage - yes, that damn word 'little' again - when he ironed his thong while still attired in the flimsy garment. Poor soul was walking like John Wayne for about a week. And I'm talking John Wayne after he had been on a month-long cattle drive.

Leaving him alone with such a lethal object as a hot iron is probably akin to requesting Sylvester Stallone, in his guise of Rambo and armed with a variety of rocket-launchers, bazookas, grenades and Uzi machine pistols, not to get upset with the antics of a few thousand Vietcong bad guys.

The subtle difference, of course, is that Rambo doesn't have to clean up after himself.

So, I have to hope I am not called away for any reason.

If so, what's the worst that could happen? Carnage, most likely. A&E here we come again. I noticed the nurses attempting to lock the doors the last time we arrived. No matter - I'll bring some flowers and chocolate along for a bribe. At this rate, I will be purchasing ocean-going liners for them before the end of the year. It'll be the least I can do.

Just so long as I don't have to hit the Prosecco cash stash. There are some things that go beyond my good nature.

LOCKDOWN, day 72

Tuesday, June 2

I presented the dweeb with a 50-piece jigsaw puzzle yesterday to keep him occupied for a few hours. To my delight, he sat at the table perplexed and bewildered until it got too dark for him to see.

How come, when I had only hidden two pieces, there were three pieces missing? I am thinking that it will reappear with the snorkel and harmonica. They were last seen in his possession. Really doesn't bear thinking about, does it?

Today, to keep him amused/baffled I have assigned him on people-spotting duties.

He is upstairs at the landing window as we speak, binoculars in hand. He has been given the task of logging those law-flouting individuals who dare to venture out more than once a day.

The poor soul is taking this onerous task quite seriously. He's wearing some third-hand full military regalia which makes him uncannily resemble Lord Montgomery circa D-Day.

You have to give him top marks with the manner he embraces these tasks. He worked his way through a full container of Brasso this morning polishing his medals (no idea where they came from - probably free with Sugar Puffs in the fifties). He also appears to be wearing my swimming goggles. Another of his lovable little quirks, I suppose.

With all those medals adorning most of his upper torso - okay, some have slipped towards his belly-button - I am relieved the weather forecast didn't predict any rain. If there had been any hint of adverse conditions with a bit of forked lightning thrown in, he could act as a conductor and be turned to a crisp in a flash. Quite literally.

And, of course, you have to take into consideration the damage that might be done to the upstairs' landing. That double-glazing cost a fortune, I'll have you know.

Once more, my apologies, dear friends and fellow-sympathisers, I digress. He has the police (not Sting and his bottle-blond mates) on speed dial should anyone be foolhardy enough to cock a snook at the government's advice. No, you don't have to be double-jointed to achieve this physical movement.

The husband had also looked out his potato gun in order to take justice into his own hands, but I dissuaded him from the notion. I reminded him of the time he was cleaning the instrument in the front garden and took old Mrs McGinty's eye out.

I hasten to add she only had the one eye hence the nickname of 'Cyclops'. She never talked about her missing orb, but there are tales of it having something to do with a limbo-dancing competition in the village hall twenty or thirty years ago.

Maybe best not to know.

In any case, I have acquired a bottle or three of Prosecco to help me through the day. One has to cope with life's constant pressures somehow, hasn't one?

And don't worry about the husband. I will alert him to the fact when it becomes pitch black and, like the good soldier he is, he is relieved of his duties for the day.

That should take us up to midnight. He'll sleep well after all that exhausting standing around.

Me? I'll maybe try to fit in another bottle of the bubbly stuff.

LOCKDOWN, day 74

Thursday, June 4

Today, I think we will wash the car. Well, when I say we, I mean I will assign that task to the husband.

I believe the drongo is wearying of all this sitting around, but undoubtedly parked on the couch is the safest place for him.

Anyway, he seems quite happy when I suggest car-washing duty. His little face lights up when I inform him he will be permitted to wear his pink polka-dotted wet suit (another purchase from Amazon when I may have been indulging in my Prosecco pastime). I noted he had been still wearing my swimming goggles from the other night when he catalogued those in the village foolhardy enough to ignore government instructions on social-distancing.

He has informed me he will be passing his full dossier of miscreants to MFI. (I think he meant MI5, but you can never be too sure.)

He looks like a movie star in his flip-flops - I'm thinking a measles-riddled Flipper. His rubber ring seems a lot tighter than it was last week. 'Does rubber shrink?' the husband wailed through grunts and gasps as he took the best part of an hour to wriggle into the apparatus.

Anyway, the neighbours have all been given adequate warning and, unsurprisingly, this has led to washings being hastily removed from lines in the near vicinity. In fact, I have been informed people in other streets (some in other cities) are also taking down their garments. Presumably, the husband's reputation has spread.

The neighbours who were sunbathing are now all huddled together and sheltering under an umbrella. It's known in The Mafia as a 'One-Bullet Job', so I am told by my friend Enrico. I must ask him one day about his apparent Cosa Nostra leanings. He's an interesting little chap who works in the local chippy. I suppose it is a bit unusual that he takes a violin case with him everywhere he goes. I wouldn't have thought that it is a required instrument for battering fish. Anyway, as the neighbours quiver in anxiety, it appears social-distancing has been abandoned, at least momentarily.

The husband is now encircling the vehicle much the way a matador would confront a bull in the ring. He is 'armed' with his bucket and trusty sponge.

I am sure that the car will not survive this robust encounter. He'll earnestly rub away the rust that has been holding it together for half a decade. The lovingly-named 'Rustmobile' will be reduced to rubble once he is finished with it.

When I next gaze upon my old partner in travel for the last fifteen years or so it will be a pyramid of dust with four wheels at each corner. The husband will step back and say something inane along the lines of, 'If a job is worth doing, it's worth doing well'.

I will make sure the old vehicle is afforded a decent send-off, and by that I mean a hearty toast with a bottle of Prosecco.

Bottoms up.

LOCKDOWN, day 80

Wednesday, June 10

Today, the husband has offered to help out at the Village Store - nothing too taxing, just a few home deliveries to the older folk who are in self-isolation.

Actually, some of the 'older folk' are probably younger than him by a good year or so, but I don't like to hurt the silly old fool's feelings.

When he went to collect the newspaper and rolls this morning, he offered his services and the owner, admittedly on the phone at the time, appeared to nod his approval.

It was quite a successful outing all round for the dweeb. He made it there and back without getting involved in a car crash or a train wreck - it's just across the road about thirty seconds' walk away - and his face was a picture. He was so chuffed with himself.

It didn't all go according to plan, of course, as you might expect. Instead of the newspaper and rolls, he came back with the Beano and a tin of spam. But, at least, he gave it his best shot.

Excitedly, he broke the news to me and was away to dig out his roller-blades. They've not been out of their box in the 40 years he's owned them, but I'm sure he'll get the hang of things after a few falls. Hopefully, he won't break his arm. Or leg. Or neck. Talk about a good deed backfiring.

He has now looked out his gear for the big day. I have removed the cardboard covering from the blades which should help him be a little more mobile and, rather sensibly, he will be donning his Bob the Builder hard hat. His trusty leg-warmers are already in place and, for reasons known only to himself, he's decided to wear a very fetching lemon tutu.

I used up all the bubble wrap when he was tasked to clean the gutters, so he must make do with elbow and knee pads. Before you say it, dear friends and fellow-sympathisers, I will make sure they are placed on the correct joints. People might point and laugh if he gets those mixed up.

The lace fingerless gloves might be a step too far, but the wee soul is so happy to believe he is contributing, bless him. I think he saw Alvin Stardust wearing something similar while performing one of his ditties on Top of the Pops circa the sixties and the husband thinks it makes him look quite groovy. I can just hear him speeding along, dropping groceries in his wake, while screeching, out of tune of course, Alvin's hit single, 'My Coo Ca Choo'. This will be real test for the collective sense of humour of the entire village; the husband crashing around, zipping hither and yon, bouncing off parked cars, thumping off anything stationery - or possibly just an unfortunate semi-comatose individual out for an early-morning constitutional - while he rampages his wayward path through the neighbourhood with the cacophony of smashing bottles echoing far and wide.

He has been tasked with delivering newspapers, sausages, eggs (what could possibly go wrong?) with the odd pint of milk thrown in for good measure. Alas, 'thrown in' could be the operative words.

If he is delivering flour, I can envisage him coming back resembling something akin to a Yorkshire pudding mix. Or, at least, the Pillsbury Doughman.

Normally, I would go with him. But, he - and I - need some space.

Plus, of course, Prosecco is calling.

LOCKDOWN, day 88

Thursday, June 18

Dear friends and fellow-sympathisers, how do you break the most chillingly bad news to a loved one? The sort of announcement that can see strong men go weak at the knees? There is no dodging the issue - it must be done face to face. I am about to impart a devastating piece of information,

I have been holding off advising the husband that our summer holiday in Crete has been cancelled. Actually, I was aware of the situation about two months ago, but I just could not find it within myself to tell the wee soul. Not at that point, anyway.

'Oh, I am really looking forward to our break, Gerda,' he has chimed on a daily, almost hourly, basis. 'Life has been so tough, hasn't it, with all this lockdown business? Not long now, my dearest cherub.' (I have no idea where the expression 'dearest cherub' came from, but I will beat it out of him some day.)

This morning, I decide to take the bull by the horns. With the days ticking down - seventeen, to be precise - I know I have to tell him. He keeps asking things along the lines of: 'Have you got the euros sorted?. Have you got the suntan lotion looked out?' Which sunglasses should I take? Will the locals still throw rotten fruit at me? Will the stray dogs still pee up against my leg?' You know, the normal sort of stuff.

I tried to get the message across subtly, mentioning that there would be no flights for months.' Alas, the dweeb doesn't do subtle. I have found the best way to get his attention is to punch him smack in the face. Repeatedly. Yes, I do realise this may come across as being a crude means of communication, but what's a little claret (as they used to say on 'The Sweeney') between friends? Needs must, my friends, and there are occasions when you have to take a short cut to making even the most

31

brutal announcement. And that takes me to this morning's conversation.

I have to say he is at his most jovial. He is practically skipping around the house as he vigorously goes about the cleaning. It is such a joy to hear him humming cheerfully to himself as he hoovers, he hasn't even noticed he's forgotten to plug it in.

I fret a smidgen before I think the time is right to broach the subject of the lost holiday. I inform him I have something of importance to tell him. Smiling joyously, he prances in my direction.

'Forget Crete,' I bark. 'Holiday's off.' I thought it best to break it to him gently.

Oh for goodness sake, I'm not a fan of seeing a grown drongo cry, are you?

The pipsqueak looks on the verge of collapse. I thought the inconsiderate little prat was about to have to be rushed to the local A&E again. I decide I must assuage him in some way, before his trembling lip threatens a tremor at the earth's core.

I manufacture a little piece of southern Crete in our back garden. He claps his hands and bounces around when I tell him of my plan. He immediately races away to one of his hideaways where he seems to secret all sorts of bizarre items. He comes back with the sort of swimsuit you normally associate with Victorian times. Remember those flickering black-and-white images of Brighton with pasty-faced individuals in a straw boater hats and twirly moustaches and legs like pieces of string with knots in them?

It isn't the buffoon's best look, I have to confess. His man boobs are not quite Page Three material, you understand. I advise him the mankini may be better served on this occasion. You should have seen the exhilaration in his little eyes. He also dug out his favourite bucket and spade (circa Millport 1958).

I remove the bowl from the kitchen sink, fill it with water, pile in a large quantity of table salt and place it in the back garden. Finding a suitable substitute for sand was tricky but sometimes I astonish myself with my own resourcefulness.

I sprinkle the patch with vast quantities of days-old dog dirt, so conveniently gifted by the local pooches around the village. To help fill it out I also add the contents of the cat litter tray. It was helpful of our little moggy to be so productive in her bowel movements (it must have been all that tuna last night). The hubby began frolicking about, splashing in the "ocean" and building an array of lumpy "sand" castles.

He looks so cheery. Smelly, but cheery.

I leave the twerp to his "holiday" while I get on the outside of a glass or two of bubbly.

I'll call him in around nine o'clock and remind him to wash his hands. I realise the back garden and poo leftovers from neighbours' overfed pets and our little tuna-devouring moggy are no substitutes for the real thing, but I figure he had had enough bad news for one day.

LOCKDOWN, day 90

Saturday, June 20

Today, we are celebrating day 90 of lockdown.

Okay, maybe 'celebrating' isn't quite the right word in these circumstances.

It's akin to falling down a mineshaft, bouncing off every sharp object while plummeting head-first into the darkness, clattering into every jagged and rugged crevice during your speedy descent and then feeling relieved when something hard breaks your fall.

Anyway, to mark the lockdown landmark, I've decided to treat the husband to a trip to the village tearoom, which is all of a ten-minute stagger from our front door. It's actually a thirty-second walk, but, dear friends and fellow-sympathisers, you know what it's like when the Prosecco begins to flow, don't you?

No need to worry on this occasion, though. There will be no carnage among the tables, chairs and floral centre-pieces while the locals, average age about eighty-five, partake of their afternoon luncheon. Of course, in these trying times, we are not allowed entrance to the rather twee, compact eatery.

I had already curtailed my visits to the establishment, in any case. I had noticed they had removed Prosecco from their alcoholic beverages. I pointed out the worrying omission to the tearoom's owner, Mrs Bottomley-Smythe. I was informed it had been deliberately taken off the menu because - and I quote: 'Some people in this village cannot handle liquor'. I couldn't for the life of me think to whom she was referring, but, suffice to say, the lure of clotted cream and handmade macaroons didn't quite appeal if they could not be washed down with my favourite bubbles. Her loss, I thought.

I have relented on this occasion, of course. Mrs Bottomley-Smythe insisted on running what she termed 'a vital service to the community' by accepting pre-orders and leaving the goods at the tearoom's entrance. The dweeb and I will be collecting our fayre of scones, cream cakes, homemade biscuits and specially-brewed Jasmine tea in little decorative cartons. I'm sure Miss Marple would approve.

Judging by the aroma that suddenly permeates the area when I tell the husband of my plan, I guess he is excited.

Bless him, he feels the need to race off to his hideaway and look out his tuxedo jacket. And he has also discovered his white shirt and dickie bow (I have removed the batteries to prevent the garment annoyingly flashing off and on at intermittent intervals). He is under the illusion the get-up makes him look a little like Sean Connery during his heydays as James Bond, though in my opinion he's missing a few small details: I'm thinking of hunky good looks, a charming smile, a mischievous glint in his eyes, knee-buckling sex appeal, and about two feet in height. Oh, and a PPK Walther pistol, of course. I wouldn't let the husband loose with a water pistol. Apart from all that, the husband is a dead ringer for 007.

As ever, in his feverish excitement, he has become a tad confused. Somehow he has managed to get his hands on a pair of suspenders and fishnet stockings. And, of course, he has a penchant for stilettos. His dress sense was never too clever, but he has not been the same since he watched The Rocky Horror Picture Show.

Actually, the last time he wore this admittedly eye-catching ensemble was at the village tearoom just before Christmas. Mrs Bottomley-Smythe and the locals were far from impressed. In unison, they rose and fired buns at the nutter. I later asked the tearoom owner why she and the locals had seen fit to take such robust action. 'We don't want to turn the place into a meeting place for freaks,' she sniffed.

Try telling that, I thought, to Mrs Wilberforce who turns up each day with her purple bloomers down around her ankles. Or Mr Barlow who hasn't done up his fly since decimalisation.

Anyway, today, we decided the husband would be permitted to wear the James Bond/Rocky Horror Show apparel. What could go wrong? He was merely crossing the road, fetching a tray and coming straight back home. I sent him on his way and went to the front window to monitor his progress. He teetered a bit on the high heels, but, otherwise, he was on course.

He was midway to his destination when Mrs Bottomley-Smythe suddenly appeared from the back of her shop. The old dear may have required bifocals, but there was nothing wrong with her aim. Or the raw power behind the thrust. Jocky Wilson, in his prime, would have been proud to claim that unerring delivery as one of his own.

The half-brick hit the husband smack on the head. He swooned momentarily before he toppled to the ground. The entire village must have heard the thud as his empty cranium made contact with the concrete.

Of course, we ended up in the local A&E, didn't we? The NHS workers, once again, didn't seem too surprised by the plight of the husband. One, though, did make an enquiry about his dress code.

'Oh, he got dressed in the dark this morning,' I offered by way of explanation. I wasn't sure if she bought that, but she certainly wasn't too impressed when I revealed he had been left sprawling in the middle of the road for about thirty minutes. Blood could clearly be seen seeping from the wound.

The nurse demanded to know why I had not rushed immediately to the aid of the husband.

'One has to get one's priorities in the correct order, my dear,' I told her.

Well, dear friends, I still had half a bottle of Prosseco to neck and I reckoned he wasn't going anywhere anytime soon.

LOCKDOWN, day 91

Sunday, June 21

Today, for a pleasant change, I have imparted the gem of knowledge upon the husband that we will be dining at the table. This is quite a dramatic departure from the norm in this household, which is the trays-on-laps-in-front-of-the-telly routine.

The washing machine is normally quite active the following day, especially if the dweeb has been indulging in his favourite chicken korma dish. Not sure how much of the Wing Wah's concoction actually makes its way beyond his thrapple, but it's fair to say a decent amount will adorn his lap by the time he says: 'Funny how you can eat so much of this stuff and feel hungry ten minutes later'.

I feel like wringing out the contents of his trousers and undercrackers, placing them on a plate and inviting him to finish his meal. Then we'll see if he's still hungry.

To be honest, I am quite happy to ensure he does not venture out today, not even for his two-minute stroll. I have every confidence he would adhere strictly to the social distancing because he is a bit of a stickler for following government guidelines. Plus he just walks to the bottom of the garden and back four times, so not too many risks being taken.

No, it's just that I have noticed some villagers congregating at a nearby corner. They appear to have stocked up on rotten fruit and vegetables. I may have detected some rocks mixed in with the cauliflower and rhubarb and the tearoom's owner, the rocket-armed Mrs Bottomley-Smythe, has provided fairly solid week-old buns that could do some serious and permanent damage.

I think the identity of the target who has provoked such considerable ire is quite clear, and that is why I will be removing the poor soul from their line of fire. Please don't call me a killjoy - I am aware there is not much choice on television at the moment and a lot of people have to make their own entertainment. I sent him out to post a letter the other afternoon and he came back covered in apple strudel. He was only gone a matter of minutes, but some of the village vigilantes - known to the husband as 'Hell's Grannies' - cornered him and let fly from all angles. I'm getting the drift he has somewhat riled the locals with his little eccentricities

Perhaps it was the nude rollerskating that was the final straw.

Or perhaps it was the sad fate of Mrs Galbraith, a portly, blue-rinse spinster who used to reside at No.88, who copied the doofus' example and thought nude rollerblading was a wonderful innovation and one day, in all her naked glory, took off on her grandkid's skateboard. Screeching the Vera Lynn classic 'We'll Meet Again' at the top of her voice, she was spotted thundering along at a ferocious pace towards a fairly steep incline - 'Dead Man's Gully' as the locals have christened it - where she then disappeared from view and has never been seen since. The police called off the search a couple of weeks ago.

I digress, dear friends and fellow-sympathisers. I have only necked a handful of Proseccos, but I'll be fine once the bubbles kick in. Now where we? Oh, yes. How excited is the pillock to be told I will be his personal chef extraordinaire today?

In eager anticipation, he has looked out his high chair and, bless him, tucked his napkin into his string vest. Why he is wearing football boots and goalkeeping gloves is a mystery to me, but he seems happy with his lot and I have learned over the years not to query some of his little foibles.

I believe he is in for a treat. I must admit, my culinary skills have come on a ton since lockdown. I used to be quite stilted with my range in the kitchen. I have at last mastered the tricky manoeuvre of boiling water in the kettle, which shows where perseverance will get you.

Excuse me, please, if I endeavour to pat my own back, but I can now cook beans on toast, cheese on toast, spaghetti on toast, pizza on toast, Corn Flakes on toast and, my speciality, toast on toast. Possibly a tad repetitive, I acknowledge that fact, but I am of the belief you must take one step at a time. In the near future, I will be moving on to eggs.

I have also mastered heating soup in the microwave. Is there no end to the girl's talents, I hear you ask? The husband is quite spoiled with this Michelin quality cuisine. Unfortunately, our evening was spoiled when he had to be whisked to the local A&E. Something to do with a blockage in his gullet.

I reckoned there might be a problem when his face turned an interesting colour of puce, his eyes practically exploded out of their sockets, he grasped at his throat, burbled incoherently and began feverishly thrashing around on the dining room floor. A bit rude, if you ask me: normally, he asks permission to leave the table.

I can tell you my nerves were shot to hell by the time I got home and I can also inform you, dear friends, that first bottle of Prosecco swiftly became history.

Well, how was I expected to know I had to remove the beans from the tin? And I don't know what all the fuss was about, it was just a small tin.

LOCKDOWN, day 95

Thursday, June 25

Today, the husband will be trampolining.

You would be excused for believing this exercise, normally a frolicking, fun event, should pass without the hint of a hiccup. But of course by now you know, dear friends and fellow-sympathisers, that there is nothing "normal" about the dweeb and thus this activity fit for toddlers and the elderly is fraught with danger and anxiety for him.

Actually, I had no intention of allowing the deranged one anywhere near a trampoline in my lifetime. I do care about the nervous systems of my aged neighbours, you know. Well, possibly not the dreaded Mrs Bottomley-Smythe, owner of the tearoom, who has been selling half-bricks at a bargain twenty pence on the understanding they are to be used solely for throwing in the general direction of the husband.

I mentioned this fact to our local policeman. He seemed extremely interested in what I had just revealed and immediately marched off towards the tearoom. I thought the old She-Devil was about to get her long-overdue comeuppance. The next thing I saw was PC McIvor beaming brightly as he walked off to his police car with a sack full of half-bricks.

Once again, dear friends, I digress. Anyway, without my knowledge, the husband was footering around on Facebook earlier in the morning. One of our kindly neighbours had put up a post saying she was giving away (free to a good home) a trampoline. Naturally, he seized upon the opportunity. I can only blame myself: I have told him to find things to keep himself occupied during these trying times. The neighbour had left the apparatus on the pavement and the husband got there just as Mrs Wilberforce was about to attempt to take it for a test drive. It is best not to consider what may have been revealed to earth-bound onlookers had Mrs.

Wilberforce bounced high into the air, purple bloomers around her ankles and skirt flying above her head.

Always the quick thinker, the husband managed to grab her by her headscarf when she wasn't looking, spin her around a couple of times, and send her thundering head-first through the immaculately-trimmed hedge. Tragically, Mrs Gilhooley's prized garden gnome was pulverised to powder by the flying granny.

Please do not get the impression the husband is a violent man. Like me, though, he has watched a few Clint Eastwood and Charles Bronson movies in the midst of countless TV reruns and, just possibly, he has picked up a bad habit or two. In any case, Mrs Wilberforce was not getting between him and his trampoline.

The dullard helpfully dragged his new toy to our back garden. I made certain the apparatus was nowhere in the proximity of anything fragile like a garage or a house or suchlike. I even moved my car to a location four streets away. You can never be too careful, can you?

Naturally, there was no way I was going to allow him onto the bouncing contraption without taking precautions. After a long, hard thought, I reckoned he might be fairly safe with his inflatable sumo wrestler's suit. I allowed him this wacky little indulgence a few years ago when we were invited to a fancy dress party.

Unfortunately, we didn't make it to the soiree. The dork pumped up the suit okay, but forgot to tuck in the valve. He was arrested for indecent exposure and whisked off to the nearby police station. Oh, how we laughed when the fuzz realised their error. They still booked him for wasting police time, though, which we thought was a tad harsh.

I kept my trusty puncture kit nearby in case of another misunderstanding. Once again, I made certain the trampoline was well away from any objects that could have been instantly transformed to debris.

To give him a good grip of the trampoline's surface, I made sure he wore his frogman flippers. As you could see, I was taking no risks on this occasion.

He had blown up the sumo wrestler's suit to its absolute maximum before he somehow managed to roll onto the trampoline. He began to bounce, tentatively at first. With a little bit more confidence, he bounced a smidgen higher. You should have seen his little face, beaming brightly before he broke into a rendition of 'I'm Popeye the sailor man.' (No relevance, dear readers, just one of his favourite little ditties.)

With every bounce, I was also able to neck reasonable amounts of Prosecco. A win/win situation, if you ask me.

It was simply exhilarating to see the husband shriek with glee as he bounced higher and higher. Up and up he went. Bouncing more and more determinedly as he grew in boldness. He almost wiped out a passing magpie at one point.

I went to the kitchen to replenish my glass, figuring I could watch him through the window. This, friends, was my mistake.

The poor soul missed the trampoline, landed on my extensive blackberry patch and punctured his fully-inflated suit. There was a loud explosion, followed by an eruption of hissing and he took off at the speed of light, hurtling like a whirling cartwheel, legs and arms akimbo, over a fence.

I found him about three hundred yards away dangling upside-down from a neighbour's tree. It took a little bit of explaining, but I think Old Man Barlow, who had yet again overlooked the necessity to zip up his fly, accepted my apology and explanation. The forgetful old soul even helped retrieve the buffoon from the groaning branch.

Thankfully, the halfwit escaped without serious injury and we didn't have to visit the A&E on this occasion.

'That was fun,' he wheezed merrily as we made our way back home. 'Can we do it again tomorrow, Gerda?'

I picked up something heavy. The wretch didn't see it coming.

I'll tell him he suffered delayed concussion when he eventually regains consciousness. In the meantime, I think I can hear that unfinished bottle of Prosecco calling my name from the fridge.

LOCKDOWN, day 97

Saturday, June 27

Today, a pogo stick arrives in the post.

Apparently, the husband thought he had ordered a pair of pyjamas on Amazon, but hit the wrong button - no surprise there, I suppose - and we've been saddled with one of the worst inventions known to mankind.

Apart from the obvious, what do you do with a pogo stick? (And no, please don't suggest that it go in the way of that missing snorkel.)

Well, the dweeb believes he has come up with a solution. He has once more raced off to his little hideaway tucked somewhere at the back of the house and come back wearing a clown's outfit. I reminded him of the last time he was attired in these same garments. The local police were called before he even had the chance to perform his magic act at the fifth birthday party of a neighbour's wee girl, Lucy. Apparently, upon his colourful arrival, the kids went screaming into the street and a couple of them, Mrs McIntosh's adorable twins, Gemma One and Gemma Two - (Mr and Mrs McIntosh were not blessed with a superabundance of imagination) - were almost struck by Mrs Wilberforce's World War Two Jeep, a replica of the one driven by John Wayne in The Longest Day.

As the hollering kids scrambled around the village frantically seeking shelter, PC McIvor arrived at 'the scene of the crime,' as it was immediately - and erroneously - labelled by our neighbours. We all know a children's party goes with a swing when there is a clown present. I know I thoroughly enjoyed my own twenty-first before I later discovered the clown was, in fact, my Uncle Trevor and that was the way he normally dressed. Genuinely, I thought the bulbous red nose was a prop.

Anyway, PC McIvor was duly summoned to wee Lucy's birthday party, which, alas, had to be abandoned after only ten minutes. The dullard, in full clown's regalia, was whisked off to the local cop shop 'to help the police with their enquiries'. As I have said, a clown can often be a memorable addition to these occasions. They add to the treasured moment and the kids, when they reach their autumn years, will be able to reflect and reminisce fondly.

Of course, the clowns are normally booked by the parents whereas the pillock took it upon himself to turn up uninvited. The daft, well-meaning soul thought it would be good for a wee surprise. Try telling that to the McIntosh twins, who are still being treated for extreme trauma.

I'm sorry, dear friends, once more I have allowed my thoughts to stray. Possibly another shot of Prosecco may assist in my story-telling. Now, where we? Ah, yes, the pogo stick.

The husband is sitting there, dressed in his clown's outfit, and has asked me to paint his face. (Yes, you are quite right, dear friends, years of frustration are about to be released.) The trusting little nerd believes I am painting a smile on his kisser, but I am copying a snarl from an image on Google which is filed under 'Killer Clown Adults Halloween Dress'. Who makes these things? Probably the same nuisance who thought a pogo stick was a good idea.

Actually, I have to pat my own back and say I did a fairly good job of the painting. Perhaps some innocent passer-by will get a fright and taser the little beggar and wouldn't that be a treat for all?

Anyway, after slipping on his size 24 shoes, he decided to have a go on the pogo stick. I informed him it would be best served if he decided to go outside after he had decimated a perfectly good lamp in the dining room. He reckoned the neighbours would not be able to identify him in his outrageous clown outfit, with his killer image adorning his face and his enormous feet.

He pogoed - is there such a word? - off in the general direction of the park before he was met with a savage barrage of rotten cabbages. The well-out-of-date vegetables rained down on him from all directions.

The rodent-featured Mrs Bottomley-Smythe, deeply-unpleasant owner of the village tearoom, had rustled up the usual vile members of the vigilante squad who appear to have a downer on the dingbat. They must have been lying in wait for hours for him to make an appearance. You have to applaud their diligence.

However, I am delighted to inform you, my dear and concerned friends, that the fusillade of cabbages did not deter the feeble-brained one from his mission as he continued to bounce merrily on his way to the local park.

I haven't seen him since ten o'clock this morning. I suppose twelve hours is a long time on a pogo stick, I'm sure he is enjoying himself. I know I am as I return to the fridge to open another bottle of Prosecco.

LOCKDOWN, day 102

Thursday, July 2

Today, I have lined up a special treat for the dweeb.

As you are aware, dear friends and fellow-sympathisers, he has been having a rough time of it recently. The dastardly Mrs Bottomley-Smythe, owner of the local tearoom, and her vile village vigilantes (try saying that swiftly after necking a few Proseccos) have been doubling their efforts to make his life a misery.

I believe they now have a twenty-four-hour watch on our cottage. I thought the coast was clear the other morning - just before 5am, as a matter of fact - and I asked him to post a letter at the nearby postbox. It's only a couple of minutes' walk away. What could go wrong?

The poor soul came back covered in jam roll. The spiteful Bottomley-Smythe must have had it on special offer. Certainly, there was plenty of it adorning the back of the drongo's napper.I also noticed a slight abrasion above his right eye. No doubt that was caused by some flying toast, fired at a ferocious rate and frisbee-style by Mrs Wilberforce. I watched from the window as she raced after the dork to pile on the agony. Who would have thought such a portly old lady could cover the ground so quickly? Especially with her purple bloomers around her ankles.

The miniscule halfwit should not take her assaults personally. Mrs Wilberforce actually has a downer on all males of the species. She hasn't been the same since her husband, Timothy, ran off with the coalman, Ernie. No-one saw that coming. The joke in the village was that Timothy couldn't resist Ernie's sacks appeal. Oh, how we laughed, dear friends. Those were the good old days of gaiety in the neighbourhood.

Not that Mrs Wilberforce saw the funny side. She was in mourning for at least a month. She even replaced her purple bloomers for a fetching large black pair. Wasn't much of an improvement, according to my husband who has an eye for these sort of things.

Anyway, Mrs Wilberforce was almost frothing at the mouth as she chased after the dingbat while dispensing wildly with the best part of a pan loaf. She was hollering and yelling much in the fashion of Red Indians in the movies before they fire flaming arrows at helpless cowboys.

Apologies, dear friends, once again I digress. Now where were we? Oh, yes, the treat for the husband. To be honest, I think the lockdown is getting to the village idiot just a tad. The other day I heard him telling a joke and that was followed by him uttering in frustration: 'Laugh, damn you, laugh.' He was talking to the microwave at the time.

So, I was doing some shopping for essentials (Prosecco) and I spied some chalk.

I think I will introduce the husband to the age-old children's game of Hop Scotch. Remember that game, folks?

We have the ideal spot at the drying area in the back garden, well away from the harridans armed to the brim with their rotten fruit, vegetables, confectionery and burnt toast. It may take the doofus' mind off the frightful attacks upon his person and it will take him ages to scrawl eight boxes on the slabs and number them correctly.

Excitement doesn't even begin to describe the wee soul's face – he is in heaven. At first, he wasn't too sure what to do with the chalk. He looked as though he wanted to eat it or shove it up his nose and, of course, some of the items did go missing. No problem, I envisaged such disappearances and bought the family pack.

He is insisting on wearing his inflatable unicorn costume. No, I haven't a clue where he bought it, either. These are what I now call my 'Prosecco Moments'. A bottle or two of the bubbly does help me get through the day.

I have explained the rules of Hop Scotch to the little nutter. He appears to have got the drift of the kiddies' game.

Just to make it more interesting, though, I tied his shoelaces together when he wasn't looking.

Well, you've got to laugh, haven't you? Why should Bottomley-Smythe and her band of shrews have all the fun?

LOCKDOWN, day 103

Friday, July 3

Today, dear friends and fellow-sympathisers, it is my sad duty to inform you the dweeb has finally snapped.

As you may have already guessed, he is quite a tolerant wee fellow. He has been running the gauntlet of the vicious Mrs Bottomley-Smythe and her shrewish crew for some considerable time and I suppose everyone has a breaking point.

Well, what happened to tip him over the edge? You could say it was a prawn sandwich too far. And something he acknowledges he will never be able to unsee. He will be required to live with this visual nightmare for the rest of his miserable existence. I feel for him.

He thought he had dodged the wrath of the village she-devils as he nipped across to buy his copy of Farmer's Weekly. He doesn't actually do any farming, but he likes to look at the pictures of cows and wheat and suchlike. (Don't ask, I haven't a clue.)

Well, the husband decided to sneak out the back door of the store after checking to make certain the coast was clear. He ventured one step out of the shop - and the inevitable happened. Mrs Wilberforce, displaying remarkable cat-like reflexes despite her considerable bulk, swung from an upstairs window. It was a Tarzan-inspired movement as she gripped onto a rope, her purple bloomers waving in the wind around her ankles as she completed the tricky mid-air manoeuvre.

In her other hand she had some inedible, weeks-old sandwiches. Splat! Her aim was true, unfortunately for the doofus. It caught him smack in the face, just under his right eye. He was so alarmed by the vision twirling around above him, suspended by a groaning rope, he dropped his prized periodical.

His look of utter fear was not helped by the fact that the purple bloomers had slipped off and set sail for parts unknown. The undercrackers flew off in a desperate bid for freedom as Mrs Wilberforce screamed and shrieked in joy, taking aim once again. Thud! Another rock-like sandwich whacked the buffoon bang on the nose. I don't know what had more effect on him - the crusty sandwiches or the sight of a bloomerless Mrs Wilberforce zipping around above his head, but I can tell you he was fairly traumatised by the time he raced home.

He was breathless and sobbing hysterically. His eyes looked as though they were about to pop out of their sockets. He informed me what he had just been through and witnessed. Sadly, he went into quite fine detail. Well, I had to pour a very quick Prosecco for myself, hadn't I? I made sure the dullard received a glass of tepid water to help him through the hideous recollection. I can be quite thoughtful at times.

The sight of Mrs Wilberforce hurtling overhead minus bloomers was what did it for the wee chap. He has been hit by half-bricks, rocks, stones, half-eaten sandwiches, buns, toast, rotten fruit and vegetables, and basically anything else the neighbours can get their grubby paws on.

He was even clattered by Elvis one day. No, not the former rock star who works down in the local chip shop, but little Millie Anderson's pet hamster. Mrs Anderson used the friendly pet - which, admittedly, has an uncanny resemblance to the crooner in his Vegas days - as ammo one day and the poor wee thing must have bounced about thirty yards after it rebounded from the pillock's napper. Well, dear friends, enough is enough. He disappeared to his hideaway and I shuddered to think how he would set about taking retribution on the baying mob that has now set up twenty-four hours a day at the tearoom.

He returned ten minutes later looking like an extra from Apocalypse Now. I don't know where he got half a tree from, but it was sticking out of his tin hat. He must have his own supply of make-up, as well. (Memo to me: Check this part of the house when no-one is around.) He looks like a cross between Alice Cooper and Dusty Springfield. Why he thinks socks and sandals complete the camouflaged look, you would have to ask him. He even looked out his spud gun and lifted a few rather large King Edwards from the kitchen store. It was clear he meant business.

The poor soul didn't make it six yards out the front door. A net dropped on him from a hovering police helicopter. The strangest things happen to that wee chap.

Later, it transpired that the thoughtful Mildred and Victor, at the local A&E, had been worried about the non-appearance of the dingbat for a couple of days. They were concerned for his safety, bless them.

They actually phoned me at home, but, alas, I missed the call. I suspect my head may have been buried in the fridge while I took care of that afternoon's Prosecco supplies.

Mildred and Victor relayed their fears to our local cop shop. They decided to investigate. They could have driven to our cottage, I suppose, but they decided to break up the monotony of a day of very little happening in the village by getting the use of the 'cop chopper', as PC McIvor likes to call it while sniggering like a naughty schoolboy.

As they flew overhead, they spied what they thought was an armed terrorist in the vicinity of our abode. With surprisingly swift reactions, they managed to organise a net and scoop up the dullard as he beat a determined path towards the tearoom. Up and up he went, screaming all the way, as the airborne police carried him across the skies to interrogate him at the main police HQ in the city centre.

However, dear friends, there is a happy postscript to this little tale of woe. A pair of oversized purple bloomers fluttered into our back garden later on, shortly after the husband's return from his 'ordeal' - his word - with the fuzz top brass. There was note stitched into the knickerbockers.

It read: 'If found, please return to Mrs Gladys Wilberforce c/o Village Tearoom'. Obviously, it was not a rare occurrence for her to shed her undercrackers. Not surprising, really, when you consider they are flapping at her ankles most of the time.

The dweeb made a tidy profit of ten quid by selling them to his pal who has a sail boat.

LOCKDOWN, day 105

Sunday, July 5

Today, we decide that it is best for the dweeb not to venture too far from the back garden.

I have taken to utilising my opera glasses to spy on activity at the tearoom where the owner, vile Mrs Bottomley-Smythe, and her cut-throat cohorts have been assembling for the past few days.

They are obviously growing increasingly restless in their attempts to inflict genuine and lasting harm upon the village idiot's person. It appears they will not be satisfied until the poor soul is an emotional wreck, dreading the thought of even venturing into the great outdoors to post a letter.

I do admit he can be a little bit of a neighbourhood pest with his eccentric ways, but I reassured them months ago that he has given up naked roller skating. Between you and me, I think he was getting a tad embarrassed with all the pointing and laughing. The final straw was when an elderly visitor actually halted his progress through the village one day and asked: 'Can you show me the way to the nearest bus stop, young lady?'

This morning, as I took up my position in the spy-hole in the top-floor attic, I saw a few of the village vigilantes testing out the sturdiness of a rope. There appeared to be a noose at the end of it. They threw it over the branch of a nearby tree, thrust the head of an effigy through it, which had a marked resemblance to You-Know-Who, and gleefully tugged the dummy skywards (the effigy, I mean, not the dork.), cheering as it swung in the wind.

At that moment, well, after I had necked a couple of Proseccos, I knew I would have to redouble my efforts in keeping the dingbat away from the clutches of these merciless grannies, these OAPs developing murderous thoughts. Cribbage afternoons at the church hall seem to lack the adventure they now so feverishly seek.

At breakfast this morning I informed the wee soul that we would be playing swing ball today (stop the sniggering, you lot at the back). He asked if we could play table-tennis instead and I had to let him down gently for two reasons; the first being that we don't actually own a ping-pong table and the second being that I didn't want any stray airplanes landing in the garden due to the buffoon frantically waving the table-tennis bats in the air like a deranged dervish. The way things are going, dear friends, would you be surprised at such a happening?

Disappointed as he was, the miniscule chap with the IQ of a drunken worm was revitalised when I informed him he could wear whatever outfit he wanted for our little game. Ten minutes later, he appeared in a full Zulu costume. I wasn't unduly alarmed by today's dress code, dear friends and fellow-sympathisers. He always did possess a penchant for dressing up and I got used to it with his mankini-and-bowler-hat ensemble which he insisted on wearing while going to the local park to feed the ducks. His little foible for costumes has accelerated a bit since he was hit on the side of the head with a rather large and extremely stale Battenberg cake. Admittedly, the colourful confectionery was still in the tin.

Maybe it was a trick of the light, but I have to admit the grass skirt suited him to a tee, the grass cuffs and leg warmers completing the look. He wasn't wearing a shirt and threw a small tantrum when I insisted that he at least don his fetching string vest which had been given a thorough wash and was now clear of most of the chicken korma stains.

I also made him leave his makeshift spear in the house. As you've learned by now, he can be easily confused, so goodness only knows where a sharp implement could find a makeshift home.

I will let him assemble the apparatus by himself – that'll be at least thirty minutes he will never get back. However, it will afford me valuable time to rummage around in the fridge for a well-earned glass or eleven of Prosecco.

I took my eye off the little rascal for just a mere moment. I returned to the back garden and there he was, soaring around the pole at a fair rate of knots. It was obvious he was extremely gleeful as he made all sorts of gurgling noises (some of them almost human). I had a fair idea where he had inserted the ball.

'Look, Gerda,' he wheezed merrily, 'I'm a superhero!'

Yes, I suppose there is space for yet another daft costume-wearing do-gooder. We've had Superman, Batman, Spiderman and even Ant-man (I never quite got that one), so why not SuperZuluMan?

In any case, he whizzed around for another three or four hours, chortling gaily as he swooped hither and yonder while I got on the outside of a few Proseccos.

The ambulance arrived around 6pm. You should have seen his little face as they whisked him off on a stretcher (with the swing ball apparatus still attached).

I've been informed the delicate operation will be performed overnight and he should be okay to come home first thing in the morning.

I'll probably leave it until early evening before I organise picking him up.

LOCKDOWN, day 115

Wednesday, July 15

Today, I consider calling in the local vicar, the aptly-named Reverend Golightly, for some assistance in the ongoing siege by the hateful Mrs Bottomley-Smythe and the vile village vipers against the dweeb.

There comes a time when you get close to the end of your tether. With me, I must admit that normally arrives around the same time as I drain my last drop of Prosecco. But, dear friends and fellow-sympathisers, I have put that down to mere coincidence.

Anyway, the poor dullard now bears the ire of the entire neighbourhood. The price of a pint of milk goes up one pence and they blame the dork. A volcano erupts in Reykjavik? Yep, it must somehow be connected to the drongo's penchant for wearing a mankini and bowler hat.

So, in these desperate times, desperate measures must be taken and I may have to turn to the church. I admit it is a bit of a last resort. I must own up to the fact that I am not overly-religious. I did go to Sunday school when I was a child, but that was mainly so I could play skipping ropes with my best friend Barbara. I used to wonder about her, though.

She kept asking: 'Do you believe in dog?' Every Sunday, she would go around asking total strangers: 'Do you believe in dog?' Sometimes she would mix it up and query: 'Is there really a dog?'

It was years before they discovered Barbara suffered from dyslexia. My apologies, dear friends and fellow-sympathisers, I digress. Now where was I? Oh, yes, Rev Golightly. Well, if you saw him glide around the village, you would realise how apt that name is. I had heard the rumours, but I just put that down to malicious gossip.

Well, I was about to put a call into the church when I espied the vicar going into the tearoom of the dreaded Bottomley-Smythe. A few minutes later, he came out with a rather heavy sack full of what I surmised to be half-bricks. I was aware they had stopped building the church circa 1760, so I had a fair idea what Rev Golightly planned to do with his purchase.

I scrubbed him off the list of possible supporters to the nincompoop's cause.

While I attempted to provide a solution, I also realised I had to keep the wee chap preoccupied. I didn't want him straying into the line of fire of the baying banshees lying in wait at the tearoom corner. I reckoned he couldn't do too much harm if I pointed him in the right direction with the lawnmower. We only have a small patch of grass and I could let him loose and tell him to simply walk up and down incessantly for about two or three hours, making sure the machine is plugged in, of course, while I get on the outside of some bubbles. Just to soothe my nerves, you understand.

He seemed excited at the prospect. A few minutes later, he came back wearing a fireman's outfit, full helmet, the lot. Somehow, he had also discovered where I had hidden his favourite stilettos. I didn't want to ask. As long as he was happy and safe - and I could have some fridge time - then I was willing to go along with it.

The numpty's wee face lit up like a beacon when he realised he was getting to use the brand, spanking new mower. I had just bought the gardening equipment at the door the other day (socially distanced, of course). The doorbell shrilled and I answered it. There was this unusual gentleman at the door: he was wearing one of those ten-gallon cowboy hats that had an arrow sticking through it. Plus he had a black eyepatch and I couldn't help but notice he had misplaced an ear somewhere along the way.

I thought for a moment he might be a long-lost relative of the blockhead - there was a bit of a family resemblance, you see. Turns out he was just a door-to-door salesman.

'Shoelaces, ma'am?' he croaked.

'Mainly on shoes,' I answered, wondering if I was involved in some sort of live TV quiz show.

'Do you need any shoelaces, ma'am?' he returned.

'Only when I am wearing shoes requiring shoelaces,' I bounced back, beginning to get the drift of this game.

This went for about half-an-hour before I realised he was actually trying to sell me something.

57

I told the odd fellow - he informed me his friends called him Humpty Go-Cart (I thought the name had a familiar ring to it) - that the only thing I required at the moment was a new lawnmower as the old one had decided to explode mid-cut.

'I've got the very thing,' he said and smiled (though it might have been wind). He hobbled off to his van. It was only then I noticed he also had a peg leg.

He peg-legged his way back with a large box.

I smelled a pig in a poke. Actually, I smelled all sorts of frightful aromas when he edged within the required two metres, so I insisted he show me what was in the container.

He struggled a bit to open the box. It was then I spotted he was missing a hand and had replaced it with a hook.

Well, he produced this wonderful, state-of-the-art mower. It was certainly the real deal. He showed me the blades and explained he was a little nervous around such sharp objects with his unfortunate history with such implements. I thought that might explain the missing eye, ear, hand and leg.

We bartered for a full fifteen minutes, but I beat him down to fifty quid. He showed me an advertisement in a catalogue for the exact same machine for £350.

Gerda 1, Humpty Go-Cart 0, I reckoned.

Now I was about to allow the duffer who shared the marital bed to give it a test drive. I plugged it into the extension lead, made sure there was power, pointed out the 'on' switch to the fool and allowed him to take over.

I returned to the kitchen and prepared to make a dent on the Prosecco stash. After about fifteen minutes, I realised there was none of the whirring sounds one would normally associate with a lawnmower powering through grass. The imbecile hadn't moved from his spot, simply pressing away furiously at the 'on' switch.

Luckily, I had kept the instructions. I fished them out of the kitchen drawer and scoured them to see if we were doing something wrong.

In extremely small print, the manual read: 'Don't use on grass.'

Gerda 0, Humpty Go-Cart 1, it seems.

Is it any wonder I am forced to take a small libation, dear friends?

LOCKDOWN, day 118

Saturday, July 18

Today, I awaken to the most God-awful shrieking I have ever heard. My first thought was that a wailing banshee had moved in next door. Remember, my dear friends, strange things occur in this village.

I roused myself and quickly realised the dweeb was missing from the marital bed. I pulled on one of his discarded Batman outfits - please don't ask - and followed the incessant roaring. It was emitting from the back garden. My empty bottles of Prosecco in the kitchen were rattling under the force of the ear-piercing screaming and I bravely ventured to open the back door. Thankfully, the bellowing stopped as I peered out.

'Look, Gerda,' said the halfwit, 'I'm a horsey.'

Last Christmas, before we were completely ostracised by the evil Mrs Bottomley-Smythe and her consortium of witches, the pillock had been asked to play a role in the pantomime put on by the village theatre group. It's actually just a collection of harmless old duffers who turn up on a weekly basis, get sozzled on homemade beer, fall over and are helped home by PC McIvor and some thoughtful neighbours. They do it all again week after week, but put on their serious heads around November when they realise something called Christmas is on the horizon and they have an annual commitment to the Festive season for the locals.

The village has performed a so-called panto extravaganza every year since the days it was legal to marry a warthog (no, I am not talking about my marriage to the husband, thank you very much you lot.)

Well, you can imagine the role they had in mind for the dork. Correct, fellow-sympathisers, the horse's backside. All thirty-two on the committee unanimously agreed he was a natural.

The look on his wee face when he was asked to participate was a picture to behold. He wasn't even put off when he was informed Mrs Wilberforce was going to be the horse's head. One had to hope the straining elastic in her purple bloomers would hold out.

Astonishingly, everything went according to plan on the night. Well, almost. The only slight blip came when the husband sneezed unexpectedly inside the suffocating confines of the costume. Mrs Wilberforce yelped in surprise, raced forward a couple of feet, and shot straight off the end of the stage. Fortunately, her fall was broken by several members of the choir. She flattened at least twelve of the children and emergency services were called. Only seven were hospitalised, but I'm told they will all require trauma therapy deep into their thirties.

In all the hullabaloo of the premature termination of the panto, the miniscule jackass ended up with the top half of the horse's outfit as well as his own bottom (if you pardon the expression so close to the Sabbath). Once again, he secreted the costume among his collection of uniforms in the room at the back of the house where even the SAS wouldn't dare to intrude.

'Look, Gerda,' the pilchard repeated, 'I'm a horsey.' Somehow he had managed to fit into the top and bottom halves of the outfit and was attempting to gallop around the back garden, much like Champion the Wonder Horse used to do in the old TV shows. The only difference being, of course, one of them was a real horse.

Once again, he made a noise he possibly thought sounded like a braying equine. In reality, it sounded more like a car screeching to an abrupt halt on gravel.

I decided to leave him to it for another couple of hours while I got on the outside of some breakfast. I raided the fridge for my first bottle of Prosecco of the day. Please don't be judgemental, dear friends, it works for me and you know the stress that I am under at the moment.

Anyway, after necking my way through a 'repeat prescription', as I like to call it - I also had a packet of mini-cheddars to soak up some bubbles - I decided to check out the antics of the drongo. I could still hear the frantic racket of the happy hubby/horsey.

Well, I found he had somehow managed to twist the costume's head back to front. He clearly couldn't see where he was going as he bashed off a couple of trees, bushes, walls, the garage, the gate. He rolled into a vast area of nettles at one point which must have been painful judging by the yelps that interspersed his whinnying.

'None of that "Look, Gerda, I'm a horsey" now, you buffoon,' I helpfully scolded the little scamp as he lost his bearings completely, thundered down the garden path and went blindly racing through a plate-glass door at the back of the house.

Well, I naturally needed a couple of shots of Prosecco to settle my nerves after witnessing that.

By the time I got to the doofus, he was dangling over the broken glass, half inside the house and half outside. The horse's head was still on back to front.

'Look, Gerda,' I heard the faintest whimper, 'I'm a horsey ... in a lot of pain.'

'That'll teach you to waken me with a start,' I said, which was about as much sympathy as I could muster.

I left him there for another hour or so. Every now and again I prodded him with a long stick just to make sure he was still with us. He grunted feebly on each occasion which I took to be a good sign although I hasten to admit I have no medical training.

Eventually, I gallantly managed to get him to the local A&E still in his costume, where Matilda and Albert greeted him with great smiles.

'We better get him off to surgery,' said Albert, showing a little more urgency. 'Maybe he has lost a lot of blood.'

He frowned and asked: 'What happened this time, Gerda?' Due to the quick turnover of our visits, we were on first-name terms with the staff.

I looked heavenwards and replied softly: 'He was just horsing around.'

Boom! Boom!

LOCKDOWN, day 124

Friday, July 24

Today, I have told the dweeb we are having a disco. He is so excited, bless him. I have no idea why. His dancing skills are reminiscent of a rhino trapped in a large balloon. A blind rhino. with rheumatism.

Anyway, he has dusted down his Womble albums. He has always been a massive fan of Uncle Bulgaria and at one stage wanted to change his name to the little creature from Wimbledon Common. It didn't take me too long to dissuade him from that particular notion, dear friends and fellow-sympathisers. The threat of extreme violence works all the time.

On Wednesday, the miniscule nutter wanted to be a movie star called Jet Thunderclap, yesterday his desire was to be an incarnation of Little Richard, but today he has settled for a more modest Disco Desmond. I can just about get my head round that.

He has raced off to his secret room at the back of the house and come back looking as though he has just walked out of a time warp. Disco Desmond is sporting his multi-checked flares, two-tone brown wedge shoes that make him three feet taller, a crazy pastel-coloured floral shirt with huge lapels and, for reasons only known to him, an Afro wig and a massive Viva Zapata moustache.I have to say it is quite a fetching ensemble. So fetching, in fact, I am compelled to raid the ever-reliable fridge for my first sip of Prosecco of the day. Can you blame me, my dear friends? I feel as though I am on life's hamster wheel with one daft adventure after another. One does need a pick-me-up every now again, doesn't one?

So, once again, to keep the halfwit away from the clutches of the vile Mrs Bottomley-Smythe and her cut-throat crew of shrews, I will set up the disco in the back garden. I know the neighbours won't mind the blaring music. I doubt they'll even hear it, as a matter of fact, as their own shouted conversations will likely drown anything else out.

They are obviously rigidly adhering to the two-metre social distancing guidelines from the government - well, I suppose someone has to - and they have been in their gardens most of the week screaming at one another in daily updates. They are bawling their heads off in what they think is essential conversation.

I have no interest whatsoever to discover Mr Jones' haemorrhoids are acting up, Mr Anderson's carbuncle is giving him gip and Mr McMillan's wife is having an affair. Actually, the last one was a little interesting because he reckons she's having it off with the Coldstream Guards. Lucky Mrs McMillan, say I.

So, I don't think some blasts of Agadoo or Wombling Free will make much of a dent on the Richter Scale around the village today.

The plonker is so happy at the thought of 'throwing some shapes' - as he has now taken to calling his favourite dance routines - that I swear his moustache has started to propel wildly on his upper lip. If he keeps getting this excited he is likely to take off and end up somewhere in Orkney. (Oh, please, Lord.)

I set up the record player in the garden and I keep him away from the electrics. You may have noticed over the past one hundred and twenty three days of lockdown he is a tad prone to accidents. He is something of a powerful magnet that attracts misfortune. It's an art in itself.

I've got everything laid out, the microphone and all the additional nonsense, but he has locked himself in the loo. I tell him everything is good to go.

'I'll deal with autographs later,' he yells through the locked door.

I feel like telling him he can take his autographs and shove them somewhere north of the tambourine, missing jigsaw piece and snorkel that have all been misplaced during recent exploits.

'I'm psyching myself up for my audience,' he adds.

Daft pillock. There will be me and a couple of curious magpies, possibly a few worms and that will be the sum total of his 'interested' gathering.

Anyway, I have every intention of spending some time in the kitchen, getting on the outside of a few Proseccos.

So, once Disco Desmond has 'psyched himself up', is ready for his adoring hordes of magpies and worms and taken his place in the back garden, we are good to go. He can get to make a God-awful racket all day, the shouty men can roar about their leaking pistons and ingrowing toenails and the like, and I can get a little squiffy. What can go wrong?

The lamebrain lifts the microphone to his mouth and screeches: 'Okay, here we go ... one ... two ... three ...'

And then he goes up in a blue flash. The poor soul is lifted right out of his wedges as he hurtles through the sky with only the garage roof breaking his fall as he thunders back to earth. He clatters the roof with such an almighty thump and a tumultuous yelp that even the shouty men are rendered silent for the briefest of moments.

I help him from the roof once I have necked a couple of Proseccos.

'What happened, Gerda?' he asks.

I try to explain, but I don't add the additional information that I was never very good at electrics and I just may have wired up the microphone wrongly. Honestly, dear friends, it was an accident. You do believe me, don't you?

I rest the drongo on the sofa and discover his Afro wig has become fused to his head. He'll probably have to wear it for the next week or so.

Ah, well, that's the way it goes. You know what they say, don't you?

There's no business like show business ...

65

LOCKDOWN, day 132

Saturday, August 1

Today, the sun is scorching out of the sky. The Cote d'Azur has turned up on our doorstep and it's time to sit in the garden, relax, maybe read a good book – and nothing more strenuous than chucking a couple of sausages on the barbecue and knocking back some Prosecco.

At least, that's what normal people will be doing on a glorious day such as this. The dweeb announces that he wants to play football in the local park, instead.

'Marble is melting in this weather,' I point out.

I swear I see his lower lip tremble. He cannot disguise the disappointment in his eyes. 'Please, Gerda,' he says, 'just for fifteen minutes or so? I promise to behave.'

Well, dear friends and fellow-sympathisers, I am not made of stone. How can I say no?

'Okay,' I relent, 'go and get your football.'

He leaps up and down with outright joy, whooping so loud it sends our feathered friends at the bird-feeder scattering in all directions.

Five minutes later, he returns from his hidden room at the back of the house. Not for the first time, I am just a tad surprised by his gear.

He is wearing an inflatable Pavarotti suit. It even has a huge head attached with just the doofus' eyes peeking out of the little holes. It's a little unnerving, to say the least. He is also wearing a massive pair of Mickey Mouse-type goalkeeper gloves. I know there must be a logical explanation.

Apparently, the world's greatest tenor was a goalkeeper in his youth. Google corroborates the buffoon's assertion. Of course, the Italian's sporting pursuits had to be put on hold when his waistline expanded rather vigorously. After putting on something like twenty-five stones in weight, Pavarotti decided it was a better bet to entertain people with incessant replays of Nessun Dorma.

'I'll go in goal, Gerda,' says the eager nutter, barely able to contain his excitement. 'You can kick the ball at me. Okay?'

I have been known to play with balls, dear friends. (Edina! What have I told you?) What I could do with balls back in my prime you would not believe. (Oh, for goodness sake, you lot at the back, not you, as well.) What I mean is, I was quite good at tennis, but I should be able to manage a football.

Anyway, I find myself agreeing with the nitwit. Fifteen minutes up at the park and outwith the clutches of the obnoxious Mrs Bottomley-Smythe and her gathering of OAP hyenas, what could go wrong?

The dork asks if I could pump up the inflatable suit and helpfully provides me with a bicycle pump. Ten minutes later, I am confronted by a full-size Pavarotti, wearing giant goalkeeper gloves and a pair of tatty football boots that have seen better days. (A bit like the occupant of the suit, when I think about it.)

Thankfully, the local park is only about a five-minute stroll away, so only one car swerves off the road as a blown-up Pavarotti passes by.

There is a small football pitch at the park with a few kids kicking a ball around. The pillock waddles past and just about squeezes himself into the goal.

'Okay, Gerda, I bet you can't score,' he says. Well, always one for a challenge, I give it my best shot. Unfortunately, the ball hit the nozzle on the suit. With a hiss and a wheeze, Pavarotti began deflating in front of my very eyes. Luckily, I have secreted a bottle or two of Prosecco in the makeshift kitbag, which helps me through the trauma.

The urchins on the field had been watching us, and one approaches me as the drongo continues to shrink. 'My name's Little Jimmy,' he says. 'I can help.'

'Oh, how can you assist?' I ask politely.

'I live just over there,' he points to a nearby cottage. 'My dad has a pump in his garage. I can get it for you, if you want. It'll only take a couple of minutes.'

I thank him for his kindness and take him up on his welcome offer. He scampers off with a couple of friends and, true to his word, returns with a small metal box. The husband is still dwindling as he stands on the goal-line. Little Jimmy attaches the pump to the nozzle, pushes a button and, amazingly, the husband/Pavarotti comes slowly back to life.

The arms shoot out, the head raises and the pipsqueak's peepers are positively gleaming. The legs expand at a terrifying rate. Little Jimmy keeps his finger on the button. Suddenly, Pavarotti is back to his full size.

I am about to thank Little Jimmy when he says: 'Just a wee bit more, missus.'

I notice his charming little smile has become a bit more wolfish.

Before I can intervene, the husband/Pavarotti/dweeb is bursting out of the goal and heading skywards. Up and up he goes. 'This is fun,' I can hear the husband/Pavarotti/dweeb exclaim. "Such fun!" He shouts again as he shoots over the treetops.

After knocking back a couple of Proseccos, I walk over to Little Jimmy who is laughing his heart out. His friends are rolling around the ground.

Well, dear friends, the little scamp has filled the suit with helium, hasn't he? You've got to laugh.

I look heavenwards and there is the husband/Pavarotti/dweeb disappearing towards the clouds. I'm sure he'll be okay. As you have discovered over the past one hundred and thirty days of lockdown, he seems to be indestructible.

I'm sure someone will return him before midnight. Meanwhile, I think I'll head back to the garden, look out the barbecue, dig out something from my Stephen King collection and put my feet up.

And make a dent on my Prosecco stash.

LOCKDOWN, day 135

Tuesday, August 4

Today, the dweeb has truly left me baffled.

Why, I wonder, is he standing in front of me covered from head to foot in mayonnaise? I know there has to be a good and reasonable explanation.

'It was Mrs Wilberforce and her purple bloomers, Gerda,' he says. I should've known the old hag had something to do with it.

While he soaks in the condiment - mainly mustard, egg yolk, oil and lemon juice, by my reckoning - I decide to pay my first visit to the fridge for a couple of slugs of much-needed Prosecco. It's early in the day, dear friends and fellow-sympathisers, but it is not every day you are confronted with your husband dressed as though he should be adorning a hamburger. In my confusion, I empty the entire contents of the bottle and suddenly the world looks a better place.

I return to the front room where the doofus is still standing drenched in mayonnaise sauce. Admittedly, he looks a little thunderstruck, his eyes are glazed and he is mumbling more than normal.

'Mrs Wilberforce and her purple bloomers,' he repeats over and over, like a needle stuck on a gramophone record - remember them, dear friends? - and I can't get much sense out of him. I spread a tarpaulin out before sitting him down, so as to avoid even more - yes, more - mayonnaise stains on our couch. You remember the miniscule cretin is quite a messy eater, yes?

Eventually, he is able to tell me his story and I remember why I married the bampot in the first place: He is a kind, gentle, caring soul. Daft as a bunch of frogs in a small bag, of course, but kind, gentle and caring.

The dork explains that he saw what he thought was an injured fox in the road just opposite the tearooms, owned by the dastardly Mrs Bottomley-

Smythe. She and her toxic bunch of crones really have it in for him and I have long feared for his safety.

Now they have added cunning to their considerable armoury of half-bricks, rotten fruit and vegetables and a variety of rocks and stones.

The buffoon, of course, is a trusting wee soul, bless him. He doesn't think twice. (I'm speaking from painful experience.) He has to investigate to investigate if the fox is hurt.

He races across the road to see if he can help the animal he believes is in some sort of distress.

Lo and behold, up pops Mrs Wilberforce, swinging her purple bloomers filled with gallons of mayonnaise above her head and shrieking like a banshee.

She has left her mangy mink stole spread out on road. The dumbbell, not for the first time, has been duped. He stands there transfixed at the sight of his portly neighbour whooping and yelling before she unleashes her cargo of condiments. Splatter! Splash! She hit the target perfectly.

The dolt stands in horror. Suddenly, the other crones loom into view behind the makeshift barriers. Stinking, months-old fruit and vegetables rain down upon him.

After standing dumbfounded for a moment, he makes a run for it.

I will never forgive Mrs Wilberforce for this act of betrayal. Back in the day - it seems such a long time ago, dear friends - we were on friendly terms, and the dunce confided in her about his heartache at losing his pet stoat.

He loved that stoat. It used to live in his hair (well, he was a bit more bountiful in that department than he is today) and he took it with him everywhere he went. (Well, he would, wouldn't he?)

I called the pet Dan - for Dan Druff, get it? I did possess a keen sense of humour once, I seem to recall.

Anyway, the dingbat was left devastated when the stoat ran off with a weasel one day. He was inconsolable for at least a month and he still sobs uncontrollably when he sees a photograph of a stoat or a weasel even to this day. He refuses point blank to watch David Attenborough programmes on TV.

The little birdbrain took up with a pet spider named Boris for a few weeks, but it was never the same.

So, I am not surprised to find that is why he is sitting now, covered in mayonnaise delivered specially - and viciously - from Mrs Wilberforce's undercrackers.

We knew there would be a simple and logical reason, didn't we?

LOCKDOWN, day 141

Monday, August 10

Today, the local police are asking the dweeb 'to assist with their enquiries'.

The chief of the village fuzz, PC McIvor, who I am aware is an associate of the vile Mrs Bottomley-Smythe, owner of the local tearoom, and her rabble of renegades, has turned up at the front door looking all very officious.

I think pressing the buzzer non-stop for two minutes should be considered unlawful intimidation, don't you?

He is displaying a sickening grin. Luckily, I have already got on the outside of a bottle of Prosecco, so I am fairly calm.

Actually, the day hasn't started well at all, dear friends and fellow-sympathisers. I awoke at around 6.30am and, after half-an-hour or so, I realised the marital bed was missing a spouse. And it was quiet. Too quiet. 'What is he up to this time, the little scamp?' I wondered aloud.

Once again, the sun was shining as I made my way downstairs. This is mankini-and-bowler-hat weather for the numpty for sure. I knocked back that first refreshing swig of bubbles and made my way to the front room. There was still no sign of the village idiot. Surely, even he is not daft enough to have ventured out the front door and run the gauntlet of the obnoxious Mrs Bottomley-Smythe, owner of the local tearoom, and her village vigilantes. Mrs Wilberforce is particularly agitated these days. Maybe she is running out of mayonnaise to pour into her purple bloomers.

I checked the loo just in case the blockhead had somehow gotten himself entrenched in the pan while 'delivering his daily sermon', as he likes to put it. Nope, no sign of him there, either.

I was puzzled, dear friends, and growing mildly concerned. I opened the back door to check the garden. That's when I heard some strange, muffled noises. Doing my best Sherlock Holmes impersonation, I followed the sounds. 'The game's afoot, Watson,' I said to no-one.

I could now detect some sort of whimpering. It seemed to be coming from an echo chamber. Undeterred of the dangers I may face, I carried on.

I spotted two feet waving frantically out of our green wheely bin. I recognised the flippers. It all came back to me then. The doofus had wanted to play some sort of 'Jaws' game last night. He flip-flopped his way to take our green wheely bin out to the point where the refuse collectors can do the needful at the back of our drive. And then he never came back. Okay, I admit Prosecco may have played a small role in my fuzziness. In fact, I hadn't seen him since about six o'clock last night.

'Thank you, Gerda,' he whimpered as I hauled him out of the bin. 'I think I got myself into a little bit of a pickle there.'

I was raging. We had missed the pick-up collection and the green wheely bins don't go out again for another fortnight.

I thought about giving him a right-hander, but I detected he was traumatised somewhat by his night with the refuse. He escaped retribution for the time-being.

And now we have PC McIvor ringing our doorbell with a rather heavy thumb as he tells me he wants the buffoon 'to assist with his enquiries'.

I've seen enough episodes of The Sweeney to know what that means, dear friends. They'll haul the little fool down to the local nick, look out the rubber hoses and then go to work on his unprotected limbs.

'Have you got a warrant?' I ask.

'I don't need a warrant,' he replies with a smirk.

'I know your game, constable,' I say putting the emphasis on the first syllable. I smirk back. I know he can't slap on the cuffs for that remark.

'I'm not here to search for anything. I merely wish to have a friendly chat with your husband. Is he in?'

'Friendly chat?' I think to myself. They've probably already got the thumbscrews at the ready. I must buy some more time. 'May I ask what this is all about?'

'It's about the vicar's missing swan,' replies plod. 'Greg hasn't been seen since last night.'

(Yes, I know Greg is an unusual name for a swan, so I better illuminate. Rev Golightly, rather remarkably, is an enormous fan of Emerson, Lake and Palmer, a fairly loud, synthesiser-led beat combo from the seventies. I thought he would have been more a Callum Kennedy, Moira Anderson fan myself, but it takes all sorts, I suppose. The band was composed of Keith Emerson, on the Moog organ, Carl Palmer on drums and Greg Lake on guitar and vocals. So, of course, Rev Golightly thought Greg would be a suitable name for a swan. Greg Lake. Swan Lake. Who said men of God were bereft of humour?)

I ask PC McIvor to wait a moment as I have left something in the oven that needs my immediate attention. I notice the dork is lying on the couch, still in his flippers, mumbling the contents of Heinz tomato soup. Bless him, he found something to read while he was upside down in our green wheely bin. I make my way to the fridge to neck a couple of shots of Prosecco before returning to the front door, where I spy PC McIvor on his walkie-talkie.

He looks disappointed. 'The swan's been found,' he informs me. 'How it got up that tree we'll never know.'

I smile a wicked smile.

'I'll be on my way, then,' he says. 'You know I will be back, don't you?'

'Next time bring a warrant, constable,' I return. Years of watching artful Arfur finally pay off.

I go back to the safety of the front room. I am delighted to see the dunce has roused himself from his slumbers and mumbles.

'I must tell you something, Gerda,' he says, looking just a little agitated. 'I have just had a bit of a nightmare. I must tell you all about it.'

'Okay,' I say in my most understanding tone. First, I have something to attend to in the kitchen. Yes, of course, dear friends, I head straight for the fridge and glide some bubbles beyond my thrapple.

I return and settle down on the chair opposite the looney. 'On you go, my pesky little chum, what's all this about a nightmare?'

'It's quite vivid, Gerda,' he says with a pained expression.

'Okay, let's hear it,' I say.

'It's all about climbing a tree in the churchyard with Rev Golightly's pet swan, Greg.'

I head back to the fridge.

LOCKDOWN, day 143

Wednesday, August 12

Today, the dweeb informs me he would like to attempt naked hang-gliding.

I have just awakened from my slumbers and I am making my way downstairs. Somehow, during the night, he has assembled something that looks vaguely like a hang-glider. Thankfully, he is not naked and is wearing his Lee Majors pyjamas (don't ask).I reckon I have a few options open to me.

One: I can immediately call the men with the white coats and request they make their way over to the cottage pronto and bring one of their special self-hugging cardigans with them;

Two: File for divorce;

Three: Check his insurance policy;

Four: Scream hysterically for the remainder of the day.

Then another alternative pops into my befuddled mind: I could crack open a bottle of Prosecco.

I hesitate for a heartbeat before I head for the fridge to get on the outside of some bubbles. I reckon they won't be the last of the day, dear friends and fellow-sympathisers.

In a slightly better frame of mind, I return to the front room to confront the husband.

'Why?' I ask.

'Why not?' comes the irritating and expected answer.

'Please, listen, halfwit,' I say, controlling my emotions. 'I only have one lifetime and I do not intent to spend it explaining the pitfalls of such activities as naked hang-gliding and other half-baked schemes that only serve to pile ridicule upon this household. Have you already forgotten what happened with the naked roller skating?'

I also remind him of the vile intentions of the merciless Mrs Bottomley-Smythe, owner of the local tearoom, and her equally-ruthless OAP vigilantes who will stop at nothing to exact retribution upon the husband.

He smiles in response. 'Up in the sky, Gerda, I will be out of reach.' The man is either fearless or possesses the brain power of a comatose gnat. I head once again for the fridge.

It's a valid point, I acknowledge as I neck the rest of the bottle of Prosecco and make sure there are at least another six bottles chilling. Satisfied, I return to the front room.

I realise being naked during this enforced leisure diversion is one of his little foibles. (Oh, for goodness sake, stop that giggling at the back of the room. You especially, Edina!)

The dork may be seen as a tad eccentric in his urge to return to nature at the drop of the proverbial hat. I ponder for a moment. Maybe he has a point. Not all geniuses are recognised at first, I accept that sad fact. Van Gogh, for instance, didn't sell a solitary work of art during his lifetime. No-one understood Richard Harris' decision to sing a three-hour melody called 'MacArthur Park' back in the sixties, but it still charted. Who could forget the vivid message from this immortal song?

'MacArthur's Park is melting in the dark,

'Al the sweet green icing flowing down,

'Someone left the cake out in the rain,

'I don't think that I can take it,

'Cause it took so long to bake it,

'And I'll never have that recipe again,

'Oh no!'

Lennon and McCartney, Rodgers and Hammerstein, eat your heart out.

Thankfully, though, Val Doonican was persuaded not to include a live version of Pink Floyd's classic 'Be Careful with That Axe, Eugene' on his 1972 Christmas TV Special.

And, of course, they all laughed at Christopher Columbus when he said the world was round. (I'm sure I've heard that phrase somewhere before. Maybe someone should set it to music.)

My apologies, dear friends, I appear to have lost the thread of today's topic. Now, where were we? Oh, of course, the husband's request to go naked hang-gliding. How could I forget?

Okay, I believe this may not be as dangerous as it may first appear. For a start, Mrs Wilberforce would need the muscle power of a female Russian shot putter on steroids for the best part of her life to reach a floating, airborne doofus with her mayonnaise-festooned purple bloomers. So, that's an immediate plus. I agree to take him to a small range of hills just outside the village. It's fairly remote and quiet and relatively pet-free.

We got to the top of a mound and the pipsqueak is already fitting snugly into his self-constructed harness. Bless him, he is all smiles as we await a gust of wind.

Sure as eggs is eggs, along comes a welcome flurry - not quite a blizzard, I am happy to report - and off goes the pillock, floating naked into the sky, blissfully happy.

'I'm freeeeeeeeeeeeeeeeeeeeeeeeee,' he practically sings.

Where the rather sturdy oak tree came from is anyone's guess.

I'm told he will be allowed to leave A&E some time tomorrow morning. I reckon I'll have enough Prosecco to see me through, so please do not be overly-concerned for me, dear friends.

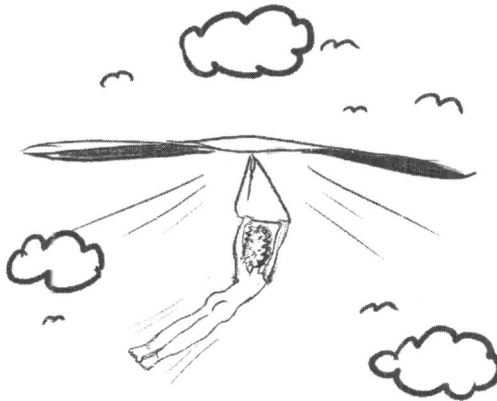

LOCKDOWN, day 144

Thursday, August 13

Today, I awake and for a split-second I believe I am re-enacting a role in The Godfather. I feel a presence beside me in the marital bed.

A hunky James Caan? A youthful Al Pacino? Or even Marlon Brando? (The Marlon Brando from The Wild Ones and not the Marlon Brando who developed into the Michelin X Man, of course.)

Nope, it's the dweeb and, for reasons only known to himself, he is dressed as Donkey from Shrek.

Instead of a horse's head, I've been lumbered with someone hell-bent on making an ass of himself. No change there, I hear you say, dear friends and fellow-sympathisers.

You would have thought the nincompoop had had enough of his equine shenanigans after his last horsey adventure in the back garden that landed him in the local A&E when he hurtled head first through a plate glass window (I am still fighting with the insurers over the claim, by the way.) No such luck, unfortunately.

The little prat must have gotten up in the middle of the night to change into the donkey suit while I worked my way through some Prosecco-induced zzzzzzzzs. I do recall he had gone to bed wearing his Shirley Bassey pyjamas (don't ask).

'Good morning, Shrek,' he smiles. (Actually, I don't know if he is smiling under that donkey's head, but I can just envisage his annoying, cherubic little smirk as he believes he is playing a hilarious prank.) My first thought is to hit him with something heavy such as a chest of drawers. 'Try smiling when a wardrobe bounces off your donkey's head, you little pillock,' I think to myself. 'Is that hilarious enough for you?'

I quickly check to make sure he has not covered me in emerald green gloss paint while I have slept. I am relieved to discover I'm the same colour as I was when I went to bed.

I try to make sense out of this fresh misery that has befallen me. Naturally, my first port of call is the fridge for what is laughingly known as 'breakfast' around these parts. A couple of gulps and half a bottle of bubbly has gone. Fortified - I said 'fortified', Edina! - I attempt to confront my personal demon.

He is standing in the front room in full donkey gear. I realise he has cracked my Amazon account code and has been piling up the orders for insane fancy dress clothes.

I wonder for a fleeting moment if the vile and vicious Mrs Bottomley-Smythe, owner of the local tearoom, and her assortment of blood-thirsty OAP crones would actually pay for me to deliver the dork/Donkey to them. I know their stash of half-bricks, rocks, stones and rotten fruit and vegetables is mounting at a phenomenal rate as my fellow-villagers make daily donations.

I could quite easily lure him into a trap. I know he trusts me (silly, little fool). I could get him in a Boston Crab, one of my favourite wrestling manoeuvres, and roll him out the front door. He'd think it was all a silly game and, before he realised what was afoot, he'd be in those OAPs' arthritis-riddled claws. I reckon I could get a tenner for the diminutive pest.

But then I remember the good times. Like the day he took me wind-surfing and was missing for a fortnight and later found in a tree in Penzance. Oh, how I laughed. Good times, dear friends.

So, I wonder, how is the day going to progress with the pillock dressed as Donkey and attempting to do an impression of Eddie Murphy. He sounds more like an Irishman straight off the boat from Limerick who has lived in Calcutta most of his life. (I'm sorry, dear friends, that's the best I can do. You would have to hear it for yourself.)

'Did you know, Gerda, that Steven Spielberg originally wanted Steve Martin to play Donkey?', squeaks the feeble-brained one. Actually, I have to confess that Hollywood snippet had eluded me.

'And he also offered the Shrek role - your part, my little tub of Haagen-Dazs - to Bill Murray? Nicolas Cage was also considered. Did you know that?'

Once again, I had to admit I did not know that, either.

'Would you believe Mike Myers was going to make Shrek's accent a thick Canadian one before he settled on Scottish?'

I have to admit I was mightily impressed by the Tinseltown knowledge of the doofus/Donkey.

I repair to the kitchen to scoff the rest of breakfast. I return to the front room armed with an empty bottle of Prosecco.

Wham! I am compelled to administer a dull one. The dingbat/Donkey doesn't see it coming. I reckon he'll be out for at least an hour.

Well, dear friends, no-one likes a smart ass.

Boom! Boom!

LOCKDOWN, day 147

Sunday, August 16

Today, I doubt if the dweeb will have to remind anyone of the two-metre social-distancing guideline.

As it is the Sabbath, I will attempt to put this as politely as possible, dear friends and fellow-sympathisers. He spent an inordinate amount of time in the thunderbox, as he has christened the loo, after he sampled a couple of mouthfuls of my curry concoction, known as Bombay Eruption, yesterday.

The Noise Abatement Society made a couple of calls to let me know they had received some complaints from alarmed folk on the Orkney Isles and they had traced the admittedly rather loud and sporadic emissions to this address.

I left him alone in the toilet for a couple of hours. I thought it the best thing to do is the midst of such a cacophony of shrieking wind and ear-piercing screams. Plus it afforded me the opportunity to get on the outside of a couple of bottles of Prosecco.

As the detonations continued, I was just relieved I hadn't introduced the doofus to my specialty dish Calcutta Explosion which is a couple of notches above Bombay Eruption. So, it could have been worse - a LOT worse. I'm a sort of bottle half-full type of gal, which reminds me I urgently require to make a swift visitation to the fridge.

Now where we, dear friends? Oh, yes, the antics of the pipsqueak and his attempts to move the cottage about five miles to the south.

Last night, as the racket faded to a crescendo, I ventured towards the thunderbox. (I don't think I will be able to call it a mere loo again, folks.) Apprehensively, I knocked on the door to make sure the nincompoop was still alive after his mighty efforts to drown out the Salvation Army Brass Band that was playing in the village green. I fear their efforts were in vain. The tubas never stood a chance.

'Come in,' he croaked.

I looked around the door. You have heard of Epsom salts as a remedy for a dodgy stomach? Well, what I witnessed was somersaults. The toilet/thunderbox had been totally redecorated.

I also spied what looked like a harmonica, a tambourine and a snorkel embedded in the walls. God only knows where the grand piano came from.

Thankfully, after I retrieved him from the bedroom ceiling earlier today, he feels secure enough and, rather gingerly, ventures downstairs.

The doorbell chimes a few moments later and I surreptitiously check to make sure it is not the vile Mrs Bottomley-Smythe, owner of the local tearoom, or any of her toxic OAP crones.

What a surprise! It is our new neighbour. I answer the door and he introduces himself. His name is Hugh. However, he informs me he is better known as Shug. (It's a Scottish thing.)

Shug tells me he heard 'a bit of a commotion' coming from our cottage last night. Shug, I recognise immediately, is the undisputed Understatement King of the Universe.

I explain the husband had a bit of a migraine and he nodded and said he understood.

However, he adds: 'I wonder if you could do me a favour, please?'

Naturally, being a helpful soul (mainly after necking a few Proseccos), I say: 'Of course. Shug. What can we do for you?'

He points to an overblown ankle and says: 'I turned it awkwardly this morning. I've got no-one to take my wee dug' – it's really wee dog, folks, but it's Shug's dialect, so I know what he's talking about. He asks if either I or the dunce could oblige by taking him round the park for ten minutes.

'Of course,' I say. 'What kind of dug is he?'

'A pug,' answers Shug.

'Oh, very good,' I say. 'And what's his name?'

'It's Duggie McDugg,' answers Shug.

He catches my raised eyebrow in surprise.

'I named him after my father,' he says.

'Your surname is McDugg?' I ask with a fair degree of incredulity.

'No,' he answers, 'it's Thomson.'

He also tells me the dug has had his daily sedative. It appears Duggie McDugg is a tad anxious around other animals. Anyway, after about fifteen minutes of banter, I agree the dweeb will go around to collect the dug from Shug.

As the poor soul staggers from the thunderbox, I ask him if he feels strong enough to take a neighbour's pet for a stroll. 'Maybe the fresh air will do you a world of good,' I say helpfully.

I would volunteer, of course, but I estimate ten minutes with the dug could see me down at least two bottles of Prosecco. I reckon it's for the best if the village idiot goes. Perhaps the pug will remind him of his long lost and beloved stoat. At the very least, it will let him air out a bit from his earlier escapes in the thunderbox. The stench might be enough to keep Bottomley-Smythe and her motley crew away.

'Okay, I am good to go,' he says. Amazingly, in the space of only five minutes, he has donned full Doctor Dolittle regalia. I have got no idea what goes on in that mysterious room at the back of the house.

'Right, then, my petite sweetness and light, just ten minutes or so, all right?' I say. 'Don't overdo it.'

He nods. 'So, you want me to take Shug's dug Duggie McDugg the pug on drugs for a walk? I won't look a mug walking Shug's dug Duggie McDugg the pug on drugs?'

With the aroma that is permeating around the dolt I could have said: 'Well, you're not likely to get a hug while looking a mug and walking Shug's dug Shuggie McDugg the pug on drugs.'

I send him on his way as I repair to the fridge. I need a drink.

So, dear friends, I reckon I'll glug-glug as the husband misses a hug while looking a mug as he walks Shug's dug Duggie McDugg the pug on drugs.

LOCKDOWN, day 150

Wednesday, August 19

Today, I awake to the garbled strains of 'fandabbydozy'.

I rub the sleep from my eyes and try to focus. The dweeb appears to be dressed as Wee Jimmy Krankie. And he is bouncing up and down on a spacehopper. My immediate thought is to close my eyes and go back to sleep in the profound wish I am merely caught in a horrible 'Alice in Wonderland-type' fantasy. I do admit to a few jolts of Prosecco late last night before I repaired to the boudoir. Or, put another way, tumbled into my scratcher.

Warily, I reopen my eyes. Is it all some sort of crazy, bubbles-induced hallucination? No, dear friends and fellow-sympathisers, it's the buffoon. Dressed as Wee Jimmy Krankie. Bouncing up and down on a spacehopper.

'Hey, you, ya deranged little pillock, what the hell are you up to now?' I shout.

'Fandabbydozy.' comes the reply.

Actually, as my slumber begins to wear off, I am stricken by the uncanny resemblance of the numpty to the weirdest comic creation since Max Wall.

He is ricocheting around the bedroom like a schoolboy on speed, his cap at a dodgy angle, the oversized jacket falling off his shoulders, a white shirt that has never been introduced to an iron, the tie undone to his navel, the short trousers exposing way too much alabaster thigh and big clunky Frankenstein monster-type boots. (No, I don't know why, either, dear friends. I have long since stopped asking these questions.)

And he is smiling his cherubic little smile while repeating continuously the word I am beginning to hate more than any other I have ever encountered in my lifetime, 'fandabby-bloody-dozy'.

I make my way to the kitchen for a shot or two of adrenalin in a bottle. I fear this may be a two-Prosecco breakfast.

The doofus/Wee Jimmy Krankie bounces down the stairs after me and continues to grin impishly.

'Can we have fun today, please, Gerda?' He looks up at me. Then he looks down at me. Then up again. And down again. Up and down, up and down. The first bottle of bubbles is drained in forty seconds flat. A new personal best.

I realise I will have to play along with him. I also see it as my duty to keep him away from the clutches of the exceedingly-cruel Mrs Bottomley-Smythe, owner of the local tearoom, and her blizzard of crones who want to inflict damage on the halfwit as they continue to seek retribution because of his little foibles (Edina! What have you been told?)Thankfully, the morning begins to settle. It is quite astonishing how quickly your senses can adapt to someone dressed as Wee Jimmy Krankie hopping around on an infernal rubber creation. (Who in their right mind invents these things? Who in their right mind buys these things? Who in their right mind wants to spend the day bouncing up and down on something called a Spacehopper? Who ... oh, I think I'll stop there.)

Anyway, as the morning wears on, I notice a fresh delivery of cakes arriving at the Village Store. Suddenly, I have the craving for a strawberry tart. (I heard that at the back, Edina.)

I mention this to the blockhead/Wee Jimmy Krankie.

'I can hop over, Gerda,' he smiles helpfully.

It's a generous offer, though I reckon he is getting bored with reducing most of the ornaments in the house to rubble during his vigorous and wayward bouncing. I decide to take him up on it. Surely Bottomley-Smythe and her Hell's Grannies won't recognise the imbecile in his Wee Jimmy Krankie guise. For a start, he looks about ten years old. (Memo to self: As soon as he starts dressing up as Chucky, the bags are packed and I'm off.)

I give him the money and tell him to get one for himself, £1.50 each and money well spent. These are the best strawberry tarts this side of the Pecos. (Or, at least, Airdrie.)

He bounces out the door and I watch his progress from the window. The nutter/Wee Jimmy Krankie knows to look both ways before crossing the road. He skilfully executes the manoeuvre. And then it all goes dramatically wrong.

'You did say strawberry tarts, didn't you, Gerda?' he hollers back from across the road. 'Not apple crumble, my sweet?'

I realise his cover has been blown. At that precise moment, Mrs Wilberforce, a woman to be reckoned with, breaks from the ranks of Bottomley-Smythe's platoon of cut-throats. She makes a Banshee-like screech as she hurtles in the direction of the goon/Wee Jimmy Krankie. She is carrying an assortment of rotten fruit and vegetables and some buns, no doubt well past their sell-by date.

The dingbat/Wee Jimmy Krankie catches sight of the harridan in full flight, thundering towards him. He takes off - or, more accurately, bounces off - down the road.

She follows in hot pursuit. Of course, the purple bloomers have now come loose and are around her ankles as she races after her bouncing prey.

A couple of cyclists stop and begin taking pictures of the admittedly bizarre scene.

The doofus eventually disappears from view, hopping around a corner. Mrs Wilberforce slows down, still half heartedly firing her missiles. It seems the drongo has successfully escaped.

The cyclists pull up their bikes at the front of our cottage. They are checking the images on their mobile phones.

I can hear them speaking. They appear to be quite excited at what they have on film.

'Why is Nicola Sturgeon dressed up like Wee Jimmy Krankie?' asks one.

'And why is BoJo chasing after her throwing rotten fruit and vegetables and rock-hard buns?' ponders his friend.

'Was it really Sturgeon?' queries the first one.

'Looked like her, that's for sure.'

'And that was BoJo, wasn't it?'

'I think I recognised the purple bloomers.'

I leave them to their conversation as they consider which news station will pay more for their exclusive snaps.

Somewhere in the distance, I can detect the screams of

'fandabbydozeeeeeeeeeeeeeeeeee.'

I know the dweeb/Wee Jimmy Krankie will be okay. He is the proverbial bad penny, is he not?

I'll drink to that. (Let's face it, dear friends, I'll drink to just about anything.)

LOCKDOWN, day 152

Friday, August 21

Today, is a red letter day in this household. We have friends coming over to visit and, no, I am not paying them to carry out this task, nor are they being marched in at gunpoint. They have actually volunteered of their own freewill to pop in for a small aperitif.

The rather large Pidgeon sisters, no strangers to the dining table, have agreed to say hello as they cycle around the village on their monthly pilgrimage in an effort to shed some lockdown pounds. I don't wish to sound judgemental, but I have to say they are wasting their time. I fear that horse has bolted, friends.

For either of the podgy Pidgeons to lose weight, I reckon they will have to have a limb removed. Or an ear at the very least.

My apologies, dear friends and fellow-sympathisers, I appear to be losing the thread of the conversation once more. We know what is called for, don't we? I repair to the fridge to help myself to some mouthfuls of breakfast which will see me through at least the next five minutes.

To save myself the trouble of another quickfire visit, I neck the entire contents of the Prosecco bottle and make sure there are other soldiers on duty, prepared to give themselves up for the greater good. I am glad to inform you six more of the platoon are poised for frontline duty. I will not disappoint them.

Now, where we? Oh, the impending visit of the well-upholstered Pidgeons who will no doubt terrorise pedestrians and pets alike as they wobble their way through the village. With a bit of luck, they will take out the vile Mrs Bottomley-Smythe, owner of the local tearoom, and a few of her toxic OAP army of crones on their journey.

The roly-poly Pidgeons, gifted the Christian names Lola and Layla by their parents, are a bit nervous of the social-distancing guidelines set down by the government.

I reassure them we will adhere strictly to the letter of the law because we don't want plod on the doorstep or worse still, another visit from the local SWAT team.

There appears to be so many people out there only too willing to blow the whistle on us. I believe the dweeb may have upset the neighbourhood to the point of no return, although I hasten to add he has not indulged in naked roller skating for some considerable time.

The little pillock cracked what he thought was a funny when I told him about the visit of the Pidgeons. 'Will I throw bread at them?' he squeaked and smiled. I soon knocked that grin off his silly face with a quick slap across the back of his vacant lot.

The lardy Pidgeons are, in fact, acquaintances of mine. As you would have guessed, they merely tolerate the quirkiness of the strange wee chap who shares the marital bed. (The Good Lord only knows my intake of Prosecco back then when I agreed for him to take me up the aisle. Oh stop that sniggering, Edina.).

Speaking of bubbles, the paunchy Pidgeons know to stay away from the fridge. There was an incident around Christmas time when I caught Lola tampering with the padlock. She told me she was looking for a biscuit.

I wasn't swayed and may have mentioned something along the lines of: 'You need confectionery much in the same manner a drowning man needs a glass of water.' I think she caught my drift.

Anyway, despite that minor altercation, the portly Pidgeons have remained fairly friendly. In truth, I think their social calendar is as packed as my own. Plus not a lot of households can cope with seating arrangements for two dumpy ladies of indeterminate age who are a tad broad in the beam.

Once I impart the knowledge of the impending visitation of the tubby Pidgeons, the doofus displays his glee (last warning, Edina!). His little face lights up like a Belisha Beacon, he is so easily pleased. At last he is spending time with people who don't want to throw rotten fruit and vegetables, half-bricks and all sorts of debris at him. It's the small things in life that keep him entertained, dear friends. (Will that sniggering at the back never cease?)

He races off joyously to his mysterious room at the back of the house to prepare for the arrival of the blubbery double-act. Moments later, he returns dressed as The Incredible Hulk. No, I don't know why, and no, I don't think I care to find out.

I plan to set out a nice tea for the dumpy Pidgeons who are as keen to get on the outside of pastries as I am to do likewise with Prosecco. On this occasion, we will settle for high tea. Sandwiches, scones and tarts. The dork informs me that he likes tarts. And then he smirks. A right-hander does the job.

Farleys Rusks for the husband. On second thoughts, they will be too noisy, I will give him watered-down Weetabix.

To my surprise, the bulbous Pidgeons arrive on time and leave their groaning bikes at the door.

They barge into the frontroom and collapse on the unsuspecting sofa. 'Hello, Gerda,' they echo in perfect synchronisation. 'Where is the little drip?'

'The little drip' in question is, of course, the nitwit/Incredible Hulk.

As a joke, while utilising his last semblance of humour, he appears at the door and announces, in his best David Banner impersonation: 'Don't make me angry. You wouldn't like me when I'm angry.' The words lose a little prowess coming in a high-pitched frequency. He roars a funny little pipsqueak roar.

Who knew the tubby twosome could move so fast? Lola grabs the nincompoop/Incredible Hulk in a neck hold while Layla drop-kicks the little varmint.

He'll be out for at least an hour or so. As a reward to the grossly overweight Pidgeons, I share a small modicum of my Prosecco.

What a laugh it is to see them collide with a lamp post as they leave the cottage an hour or so later.

I hear the dweeb/Incredible Hulk begin to rouse himself on the floor. Carefully, I step over him on my way to the fridge for some celebratory bubbles.

LOCKDOWN, day 155

Monday, August 24

Today, I awake to the less-than-melodious strains of 'The Pied Piper', that irritating sixties' pop ditty song by the nerdy Crispian St Peters.

I have warned the dweeb in the past about putting this annoying record on his personal turntable. I thought revealing Crispian St Peters' real name of Robin Peter Smith - yes, honestly - might strip away some of the mystique of this so-called Hit Parade performer. Alas, as I have just discovered, my efforts have been in vain.

'Hey, come on babe, Follow me, I'm the Pied Piper,

'Follow me, I'm the Pied Piper, And I'll show you where it's at.

'Come on, babe, Can't you see, Trust in me,

'I'm the Pied Piper, And I'll show where it's at.'

The infuriating and repetitive music drifts upwards from the front room and attacks my senses. Even more worryingly, this is before my first jolts of Prosecco. (Memo to self: Insert mini fridge beside bed.)

'Hey, come on, babe, Follow me, I'm the Pied Piper ... '

(My apologies, dear friends and fellow-sympathisers, if those words are stuck in your head for the rest of the day.)

In a way I blame myself for the drongo's actions. As I step over his discarded Forrest Gump pyjamas (don't ask) on my way to the kitchen for some vigorous fortification - I said 'fortification', Edina and you sniggering lot at the back - I remember the little pillock taking an interest in a couple of books I had looked out from my collection last night.

I noticed he had taken a particular interest in Robert Browning's story about a rat-catcher in the German village of Hamelin who somehow lured away disease-riddled rodents by playing the pipes, thus saving everyone from an epidemic. Where is he now when we need him?

The story goes that the villagers didn't pay him and the slightly-miffed Pied Piper returned and lured their children away too, but that might be a tad dark to contemplate at this time of the morning.

Anyway, as you would imagine, the drongo wasn't actually reading the book - that's a stretch too far - but he did seem engrossed by the illustrations.

You can see where this is going, can't you?

I head for the fridge and fire a couple of jolts of Prosecco, bracing myself for whatever fresh horror awaits me. With trepidation, I open the door to the front room. What I'm met with is worse than I could have imagined.

The pipsqueak has dug out my old tartan mini-skirt (my legs didn't always resemble overgrown chipolatas, I'll have you know). He has also adorned himself with a matching tartan jacket and found some sort of headgear that looks as though someone has squashed a multi-egg omelette on his vacuumed napper. Naturally, he has set off the look with his favourite pair of red wellingtons.

I don't recall ever seeing illustrations of the Pied Piper of Hamelin quite dressed in such a zany manner, but, hey, the buffoon has allowed his creative juices to flow (and not before time, I hear you say in pity).

"I am the Pied Piper,' the little pillock announces. He is just about to hit the replay button for the Crispian St Peters jingle again when he catches my expression. Sensibly, he withdraws.

'I am the Pied Piper,' he repeats and adds, 'and I'm going to save the town.'

Bless him, the wee soul seems to have gotten confused and thinks the virus keeping us indoors is being caused by rats. It is never a joy to dash someone's dreams, but I feel duty-bound to let the village idiot down gently.

'Please listen to me, my little hell on earth,' I say in my best lilting tones, 'the only rats in the village are Mrs Bottomley-Smythe and her vile assortment of OAPs who are thirsting for blood. They haven't got near you for ages and they are getting anxious. One sight of you and they will tear you limb from limb before setting fire to your face.'

The little dork laughs.

'I smile in the face of menace,' he says. (He's been watching Clint

Eastwood/Charles Bronson movies again, I realise.) 'Danger is my middle name.'

'Danger'? I would've guessed 'Drongo'.

I repair to the fridge. It is obvious he is not going to be dissuaded from today's crazy crusade. And he has gone to some considerable effort in putting together his 'Pied Piper' costume.

When I return to the front room, the husband/Piped Piper/ little pipsqueak has suddenly produced a clarinet (now where did he pull that from?).

'I'm going to save the town,' he says again and prances out the door.

I watch from the kitchen window as he picks up a bird feather stuck in some sort of goo and inserts it into his omelette/hat. Then, he brings the clarinet to his lips and begins to play.

Well, perhaps 'play' is too kind a word. The man is obviously self-taught, dear friends. No, the sounds he produces from the instrument are more akin to a rabid cat being stuffed in a bag and swung around. So horrifyingly ear-splitting is the doofus' music, that it immediately sets off some howling from agitated neighbourhood dogs. A second later, a pack of the canine beasts burst through a garden hedge and begin tearing after the piper/nincompoop. Duggie McDug the pug is leading the pack, nipping at the dork's heels.

The cretin continues to prance and play, tartan mini-skirt flapping in the wind. It seems he has forgotten his undercrackers. I watch until he and his canine entourage disappear around the corner, never to be seen again.

Oh, I'm only kidding. But one can dream, can't one? And I shall continue to dream while I repair to the fridge and crack open another bottle of Prosecco.

LOCKDOWN, day 158

Thursday, August 27

Today, I awake to the dulcet tones of Shirley Bassey. 'Diamonds Are Forever' is cascading around the cottage and my immediate thought is: 'What is the dweeb up to now?'

My second thought is altogether more pleasant. I wonder if it is an anniversary and a special day awaits.

And then I remember the little drongo who took me up the aisle (oh, for goodness sake, you lot at the back) and I recall he doesn't do anniversaries.

The alarm clock tells me it is just 7.46am. Well, it doesn't actually tell me it's 7.46am, of course. The digital numbers show me it's 7.46am. Well, it doesn't actually show me it's 7.46am, either, when I think about it. The numbers are arranged in such a manner I can work it out for myself that it is 7.46am. Well, it's now 7.47am. I think I better get up. Above the lyrics of Ms Bassey, the song of Prosecco is calling me.

I step over the drongo's Ursula Andress pyjamas (don't ask) and head downstairs. A few jolts of the suds do the trick. Fortified, I am ready to face the rigours of another day with the miniscule dork who shares the marital bed.

I open the front room door. Dear friends, I think my jaw literally drops.

'Good of you to join ush, Mish Moneypenny.'

I am speechless (which is unusual after just one bottle of Prosecco, dear friends and fellow-sympathisers).

'I shee you have come to join ush.'

I turn on my heels and head to the fridge for a second bottle of bubbles. I get the feeling this might be a long day.

I return and hope my tired, old eyes have been playing tricks on their

99

owner. No, the little pipsqueak is still standing in the middle of the room. He is wearing a white tuxedo jacket with a 'gift' from a passing seagull still visible on his left shoulder. I told him not to wear that jacket outside, but would he listen to good advice? (Answers on a £10 note, please, to the usual address.)

He has been rummaging around again in that room I dare not enter and has found a bow-tie. It's not a bow-tie you would ever see adorning the neck of James Bond, though. This one is straight from Coco the Clown and is flashing on and off. It's not a good look.

I note he is also wearing a pair of my Aunt Matilda's old leggings. They are grey, wrinkly, sagging and falling apart (a bit like my Aunt Matilda when I come to think about it). I have no idea how he got his hands on them. Best not to ask for fear of getting an answer, dear friends.

Of course, he is wearing a pair of sandals and his socks with the little puppies. He never has got the hang of this dressing up caper, has he? I notice Claude, the family cat, is hiding behind the sofa.

And the husband/007/village idiot is caressing his well-worn spud gun. Oh Edina! Control yourself you lot. I, of course, am referring to the spud gun he attempted to fire at cyclists what seems like an aeon ago.

'Okay, what this all about, you little madman?' I ask.

'Well, Mish Moneypenny, I can't shay I like your tone, for a shtart,' he says, caressing the spud gun.

'Why are you playing Diamonds Are Forever so loudly at this time in the morning?' I ask reasonably.

'I have never heard of shuch a shong, Mish Moneypenny,' he replies.

'What do you think you are listening to just now, you little pipsqueak?' I practically shout in exasperation.

'There ish no shuch record, Mish Moneypenny.'

'Are you deaf?' I scream. 'That's Shirley Bassey singing Diamonds Are Forever, is it not?'

'A common mishtake,' he smiles. 'That ish, in fact, Shirley Basshey shinging Diamondsh Are Forever.' Very shimilar, but not quite the shame.'

'And who are you supposed to be?' I decide to play along before I lose my mind completely.

'I'm Bubble Oh Sheven,' he smirks that annoying smirk. Or, as he

100

would undoubtedly say: 'He shmirksh that annoying shmirk."

'Don't you mean 007?' I ask.

'No, Mish Moneypenny, I mean Bubble Oh Sheven. I'm jusht out of the bath, you shee.'

I say nothing. I realise I have entered another circle of Dante's Inferno.

He stands there, rubbing his spud gun (Edna! Quiet now!), the bow-tie flashing off and on, the bird dropping quite apparent on the shoulder of the white tuxedo, my Aunt Matilda's old baggy leggings, sandals and puppy socks.

And you wonder why I drink, dear friends?

I reckon another few jolts - well, a bottle, if I am being honest - is required. Urgently.

I return to the front room. He is still grinning inanely. 'I shee you are not wearing any pantiesh, Missh Moneypenny,' he says.

I decipher that quickly in my head. Did he really say: 'I see you are not wearing any panties, Miss Moneypenny'?

He catches my quizzical expression and shows me his watch. (It's an old Mickey Mouse wristwatch he got out of a lucky bag about fifty years ago.) 'I am jusht teshting thish new watch I rechieved from M thish morning,' he says. 'It informsh me you are not wearing any pantiesh, Mish Moneypenny.'

'Well, 007, I can tell you it is faulty,' I retort. 'I am, in fact, wearing panties.'

The doofus/James Bond looks again at his watch. 'Damn, the bloody thing ish an hour fasht,' he says.

He didn't see it coming. The empty bottle hit him smack on his black wig. Down he went in a heap. It was a direct hit and I was quite pleased with myself.

'Well, that will be the end of this little charade, Mr Bond, for a couple of hours, I think.'

I head for the fridge.

'Bring on that Prosecco, Mish Moneypenny hash worked up a thirsht,' I shay to myshelf

LOCKDOWN, day 160

Saturday, August 29

Today, I awake and I am immediately filled with fear and trepidation. No, there is not a severed horse's head lying beside me as a gift/warning from the local mafioso, though I'd not put it past the vile Mrs Bottomley-Smythe, owner of the local tearoom.

Well, I go to bed with a horse's backside every night, so why bother about waking up with another part of the animal's anatomy? Yes, dear friends and fellow-sympathisers, I get your point and I applaud you for your astuteness.

A horse's head I could handle. No, what fills me with so much unease this morning is the sound of music emanating from the kitchen. Yes, that's right: the kitchen, the site of my most prized possession - a fridge full of Prosecco.

Two days ago I awoke to 'Diamonds Are Forever' from Shirley Bassey. Today, the dweeb, Tony Blackburn has put something entirely different on the turntable.

The Stripper.

And we are not talking DIY background music, dear friends.

It's the full bump and grind belter made so infamous in those sort of shady, sordid nightclubs we don't mention over tea and tiffin at the sewing bee (whatever a sewing bee is).

You must have heard it, dear friends and concerned colleagues. It normally plays to the accompaniment of one of those ridiculously lithe and well-endowed females who appear to have all their parts in the right place. We can't all be so lucky.

As I step over his Jack Palance pyjamas (don't ask), I swiftly get dressed and prepare to go downstairs. It's in moments like these, dear friends, I

103

wish I kept an Uzi machine gun under the bed for such emergencies.

The music reverberates off the walls, bump and grind, bump and grind. 'What is the little nerd up to?' I ask myself. 'Surely, he isn't in training to be a hustle bunny?' (I picked up that term from an old episode of Dragnet.)

I really do not think I can stomach the thought of a naked dork cavorting around the cottage so early in the morning. Especially, as I have not had my customary few jolts of Prosecco. And the Good Lord only knows where he would put those tassels. You know the ones that these voluptuous-type of females adorn strategic parts of their upper torso with while they go through their rather tawdry routine, divesting themselves of their clobber. Not that they begin with too much on in the first place. (So I have been informed.)

The music gets louder as I head for the kitchen. What awaits me behind that door?

Normally, this is a happy moment of the day, my breakfast introduction to the bubbles. As you are aware, dear friends, I do require a good fortification in the morning (oh, for goodness sake, Edina and you lot at the back, this is serious).

But what awaits me on this occasion? What horror is about to be presented before my very eyes?

Bump and grind, bump and grind.

Bravely, I push open the door.

Bump and grind? It's more shake and bake.

The husband/little drongo is dancing away merrily in the middle of what I can only describe as an explosion in a chicken coop. There is yolk dripping from the ceiling, egg shells are stuck to the walls, you can barely see through the windows. (Not that they were pristine, anyway, I must confess.) The little madman has covered the kitchen in produce from our little clucking - I said 'clucking', Edina - feathered friends.

Thankfully, he is fully clothed. I notice he is wearing an outsize pair of spectacles he picked up on a school holiday in Blackpool back in the day before fire was invented.

Before I get the opportunity to pop a cork - that's not a euphemism for anything, I hasten to add - he turns to me and cries: 'Wheeehay, it's little Ern. I thought I would rustle up some breakfast, my short, hairy-legged amigo.'

The penny drops. The miniscule knucklehead has been watching the Morecambe and Wise Christmas Special from 1978 again, hasn't he? The one that has Eric and Ernie making breakfast in perfect synchronisation to the strains of The Stripper. (Ahh, the good old days.)

Anyway, his re-enactment of the comedy cameo has not gone quite according to plan. 'I was going to make bacon and eggs, my little bewigged friend, but I think it will now be an omelette.' He then wiggles his spectacles (I said 'spectacles', Edina).

What's a gal to do? I reck a bottle of Prosecco pronto and administer a dull one with the empty bottle. As I swipe the bottle off the little nincompoop's empty napper, I open another with my free hand. Now that's what I call co-ordination.

I reckon he'll be out for about an hour or so. I leave him lying in the debris of what looks like the aftermath of a crash involving a truck carrying 10,000 eggs.

It is at this juncture, dear friends, I have a confession to make and I do sincerely hope you do not think badly of me when I divulge this information.

I admit I did have an attempt at Pole dancing in my far-off youth.

Apparently, he fled back to Warsaw the following day.

LOCKDOWN, day 164

Wednesday, September 2

Today, I am going to put the yay into the day, so it's hooray I say to bubbles all the way from Ita-lay. (Okay, it's not quite Poet Laureate material, but please cut me some slack, I've just woken up.)

I am determined to go through today with a smile on my face, irrespective of the inevitable irritations that will come my way from the husband/little doofus.

It takes me fifteen minutes or so to get my focus after a night out with Johnny Weissmuller (the original Tarzan for some of my younger friends and fellow-sympathisers). We had a wonderful time swinging through the jungle. Oh, for goodness sake, you lot at the back, this is 'swinging' in the old-fashioned way: gripping vines as we sweep from tree to tree. Not that other sort of 'swinging' I read about these days where people certainly don't observe the government's social-distancing guidelines. They don't seem to adhere to any sort of guidelines, when I think about it.

In my dreams, Tarzan swings his way back to our tree hut after a day at the office. (He's got all sorts of awards in accountancy, a little-known fact about Edgar Rice Burrough's fictional character.) The King of the Apes has got a good sense of humour, another wee gem of info.

Every day when he gets home I pour him a dry Martini. I know he enjoys relaxing when he gets home because he always says: 'Gerda, it's a jungle out there.'

Apologies, dear friends, it did make me snigger. Admittedly, I had already got on the outside of some liquid inspiration by then.

Other girlfriends get cuddly toys, I get the real thing. At last count in my fantasies, I had about five lions, two gorillas and a tiger. It is a tad cramped in our accommodation and a smidgen whiffy, but I have to say in my defence I have no control over what happens when I close my peepers after a Prosecco-fuelled day.

I am now properly awake and I throw my legs - and the rest of my body - out of what is laughingly known as the marital bed and make sure I do not stand on the husband's Linda Lovelace pyjamas (don't ask). I won't got into details, dear friends, but I have to say the designers have shown some imagination with this production. I think I'll leave that there, if you don't mind.

Anyway, I head down to the fridge for what I now term my 'Jump-Start Juice' aka Prosecco. I fire a couple of jolts behind my necktie and suddenly the world looks a better place. What on earth do those clever Italians cram into these bottles?

I take my morning trek through to the front room, push open the door and I am confronted by The Joker from Batman. Well, of course, the husband/little dork appears to be celebrating lockdown day 164 and he feels the need to be dressed as the Caped Crusader's arch-enemy. I don't really want to ask, but I can't help myself.

'Why are you in the guise of a hideous character from Gotham City?' I enquire.

'I have been told I must wear a mask,' he replies.

I am taken quite by surprise, dear friends. Another couple of shots of suds are called for. Urgently. I make my way back to the fridge for much-needed fortification. (Yes, Edina, I did say fortification.)

I have never known the little pillock to take any interest in current events. In our early days, he used to buy the Daily Express every day and I had to ask him why that was his favourite newspaper? Was it the sharp reporting, the politics, the interesting interviews, the features or even its sports coverage.

'Rupert The Bear,' he informed me and I should have known why it took him only two minutes to 'read' the journal before discarding it.

Somehow the little dweeb has picked up the thread of what Nicola Sturgeon, Wee Jimmy Krankie as some call Scotland's First Minister, has been urging the nation during these dark pandemic days.

I am so impressed I knock back another bottle of bubbles. (Yes, I know, dear friends, I am fairly easily impressed.)

Now that he is wearing his mask, I decide to put it to a good use and ask him to go over to the Village Store for a Radio Times, a Farmer's

Weekly (for him) and a couple of fresh rolls. I realise he'll probably come back with a loaf, a couple of sausages and a toilet roll, but, hey!, it is Wednesday, so let's live dangerously. (Is there any other way, dear friends?)

The doofus/Joker is up for the task. I pass on the correct money and tell him to watch out for the vile Mrs Bottomley-Smythe, owner of the local tearoom, and her motley crew of odious OAPs who still have him as Public Enemy No.1 on their hit list.

'Batman and Robin are wasting their time, my little cherub,' he laughs, 'The Joker is way too smart for them.'

I nod my head. I am in this movie every day and, as you know, Prosecco is my main ally. I make a small adjustment to his equipment (I adjusted his mask, Edina! Wipe that smirk off your face) and send him on his way.

He is only about twenty seconds out of the door when I hear the whoops and howls of the dreaded Bottomley-Smythe and the treacherous Mrs Wilberforce, purple bloomers at her ankles, as they spot the little dullard make a rare public appearance.

They see through his Joker disguise immediately.

Suddenly, there is a blizzard of rock-hard buns raining down on the pathetic little creature as he yelps and scurries off down the road with a posse of Hell's Grannies shrieking and screaming as they give chase.

I repair to the fridge, chuck a couple of slugs behind my thrapple on their way to Happy Valley. And I smile. My slight adjustment to his mask has worked a treat. He might have got away with the disguise if the grinning face had been the right way around. Somehow, though, it has worked its way to the back of his head.

The little simpleton's face is exposed and then the party kicks off. Oh, such fun.

I've had the last laugh on The Joker. (Apologies.)

LOCKDOWN, day 165

Thursday, September 3

Today is a day of high drama in the village. No, they haven't brought back burning witches which is good news for the vile Mrs Bottomley-Smythe, owner of the local tearoom, and her collection of deranged, toothless crones.

Nor have they given the go-ahead for public flogging. A bit of a shame, really, because I used to enjoy some poor wretch being lashed to within an inch of their worthless life on a Thursday evening (particularly when there was nothing on the television).

Public floggings were banned a few years ago. The village is struggling to catch up with the 18th Century.

Nothing wrong with a little flagellation (oh, please, you lot at the back) for someone caught fly-tipping or not cleaning up after their pet pooch has left a creation the size of Annapurna on your front lawn.

No, dear friends and fellow-sympathisers, nothing quite as exciting as that, I'm afraid. The husband/little dweeb escapes for another year.

Today - drum roll, please - is the day of the annual Scarecrow Competition. It has become a tradition in the village for households to construct their own effigies and display them in their gardens.

It's all a bit of fun - and the Good Lord knows we could all do with that precious commodity on day 165 of lockdown - but it has become exceptionally competitive over the years. (One judge was thought to have been bribed with a year's supply of tinned spam if she favoured the village store's exhibit a year or so ago. There is corruption in high places everywhere, dear friends.)

My own offering this year was one of Donald Trump. It actually only took me about five minutes to construct. I had a few mattresses in the

109

garage rotting away and I merely stuffed them into one of the husband's suits, planted a rather large orange balloon where a head should be and threw an old mop on top. Well, the resemblance was just uncanny.

However, it pains me to tell you that Donald disappeared a few nights ago. There have been unconfirmed reports that Mrs Wilberforce, with her purple bloomers around her ankles, of course, was spotted walking down the street hand in hand with Donald.

According to one onlooker, they looked quite a well-matched couple. I'm not sure who I feel more sorry for. (Donald probably edges it.)

Anyway, dear friends, to help me through the day I will have a little foray towards the fridge for a bottle of breakfast to steady my nerves on this momentous occasion for the village.

I clamber out of bed, making sure I do not step on his Mae West pyjamas (don't ask) and head for the suds. A few jolts of Prosecco - well, a bottle and a half, if we are searching for accuracy - and I am ready for the rigours of another day at the coalface of life.

The husband/little pipsqueak is already standing looking out the front window. He has probably exhausted his conversation with the vase he believes to be a parrot.

'This is exciting, Gerda,' he squeaks.

Well, it is about as exciting as it gets around these parts, folks, especially in these confined times. Anyone with a passing resemblance to Jon Pertwee is almost guaranteed a place in the top three.

The winner will be announced at High Noon. The first prize is lunch at the obnoxious Mrs Bottomley-Smythe's tearoom. The second prize is a stomach pump for the winner of the first prize. Third is a choice of bed at the local A&E for the winner of the first prize if the second prize doesn't do the job.

Well, it's all very tense before the victorious dummy is revealed. However, there appears to be a bit of a mix-up in the judging, dear friends.

The triumphant ragamuffin is paraded as the effort from Mrs Thompson who has constructed the most wonderful image of a drunken lady, festooned with bottles and sitting in her purple wheelie bin, with a large sign on the scarecrow proclaiming it to be 'Lucy The Lush'.

It is exceptionally well done and extremely lifelike. They are about to pin on the winning rosette when 'Lucy The Lush' comes to life. It appears

Mrs Thompson had merely gone for her late morning nap and had been picked up by one of the volunteers who rounded up the exhibits.

They gave her first prize, anyway.

LOCKDOWN, day 168

Sunday, September 6

Today, I awake, which, all things considered, is a reasonable start to the day.

It gets even better when I realise there is no sign of the husband/little pest. With a smidgen of good fortune, a golden eagle has possibly come in the middle of the night, removed him from the marital bed and taken him off to a mountain top in a far-off land. I realise that is probably too much to hope for. A gal can dream.

Undeterred, I swing my legs out of bed and make my way past the discarded Boris Karloff pyjamas (don't ask).

'So far, so good,' I say to myself.

There was a strange giant orange orb floating in the sky yesterday. I have been informed in the past this phenomenon is something that is often referred to as 'the sun'. We do not often witness this astonishing spectacle in our corner of the universe.

However, I had mentioned to the little dweeb we could arrange a barbeque in the back garden, once again keeping the village idiot away from the clutches of the vile Mrs Bottomley-Smythe and her band of OAP cut-throats known as Hell's Grannies.

They have never forgiven the diminutive numbskull for a variety of so-called offences, one being his naked roller skating through the neighbourhood. Frankly, dear friends and fellow-sympathisers, I don't understand what the fuss is about. And I should know. But enough of my personal heartache.

Yes, I could allow the little drongo to be whisked away by the baying crowd that sets up every day outside the local tearoom and howl for blood, with their rock-hard buns at the ready. (Not a pretty sight, as you could well imagine, dear friends.)

However, I could never forgive myself if the little halfwit ended up as one of the untrustworthy Mrs Bottomley-Smythe's 'Special Sunday Roasts'.

As I open the curtains before this morning's main business - getting on the outside of a bottle of breakfast, of course - I realise all hopes of a barbeque in the back garden have been extinguished. The orb is gone, grey clouds have gathered, and there is a steady drizzle. It was nice while it lasted.

All is quiet as I head for the fridge and its welcoming contents. I fire a couple of jolts of Prosecco behind my neck-tie. And then a few more. Before you know it, dear friends, the contents have mysteriously vacated the container. The solution, naturally, is to open another to make sure it is at the right temperature. A couple of glugs later and I can now confront a new dawn in the hell that is my wretched life.

I push open the door to the front room and I am confronted by the Dork with a Fork. (No sniggering at the back, please.)

The little dumbbell has prepared for a barbeque. I suppose he hasn't noticed the torrential rain.

As I look at the miniscule chump standing there, I have to admit to a small pang of sorrow. (Just a small one, mind you.) The deranged buffoon has actually dressed for the part, apparently modelling his costume after the Swedish chef from The Muppets.

'Voordy voo, Gerda,' he says.

Naturally, I am rendered speechless. I repair immediately to the fridge for a few more necessary slugs of the bubbles.

'Hurdy gurdy, Gerda,' he says when I return. I can just about detect his irritating little smile.

Of course, my natural instincts are to administer a dull one. Who could blame me? He is standing there, holding an enormous wooden fork in one hand and an equally large wooden knife in the other.

He is wearing a pillow on his head. It's stuffed with something to keep it upright and I wonder what is in the headgear. I realise I have not seen Claude the cat today.

He has looked out his Charlie Chaplin baggy trousers and has found an old apron of mine from somewhere. It is covered in mince and I wonder what I was making the last time I wore it. Another mystery that will never be solved, dear friends.

He is also wearing a pink bow-tie that lights up every ten seconds. On the plus side I can hardly see his face. He has attached two strips of carpet to his eyebrows and, with the same material, to his upper lip. I can't help wondering if it will be painful when I rip off the eyebrows and moustache. The enticing thought warms my heart for a fleeting moment.

'Voordy voo,' he repeats from under the facial adornment that started life as a fireside rug.

'Hurdy gurdy,' he adds swiftly.

He clatters the wooden utensils together.

'See de moofin?,' he says and I realise he has been up most of the morning practising Swedish. 'Und here de boom-a-shootin.'

I say nothing, dear friends. It has got nothing to with the effects of two swift bottles of Prosecco, I hasten to add.

'Bork, bork, bork,' he gibbers, quickly adding, 'Voordy voo, hurdy gurdy, Gerda.'

He thumps the giant wooden fork and knife together again.

I apologise, dear friends, but that was the moment I lost reason. Guess where the over-sized utensils were deposited? Yes, you would be right.

The husband/Swedish chef/little dingbat will be walking funny for the rest of the week. The local A&E may have to be called in at some point.

'Voordy voo to you, too,' I grin and head for the fridge.

Please watch out for a Swedish chef with a strange gait.

LOCKDOWN, day 170

Tuesday, September 8

Today, my pleasant reverie and enjoyable dreams of swanning around Prosecco Paradise (my special place) have been obliterated by some raucous screeching that sounds like a constipated elephant giving birth.

Of course, I doubt if this is the case. We don't get too many of the largest existing land animals - constipated, pregnant or otherwise - wandering uninvited around our front room.

If there had been any such distinct and colossal mammal in the vicinity last night, I'm sure I would have noticed. Okay, I admit the bubbles had been going down fairly well and I may have gone into double figures on the bottle count, but, hey, it's not every day September 7 2020 comes around. (A genuine one-off occurrence, when I think about it.)

As my peepers adapt to a new dawn in hell, I swing my legs out of the marital bed and I make sure I do not step on the discarded Father Ted pyjamas (don't ask).

They are the little dweeb's special night-time attire that make an appearance once a year to commemorate the Eurovision episode of the TV comedy. Do you remember it, dear friends and fellow-sympathisers?

The one where Father Ted and his imbecilic clergyman sidekick, Dougal - remind you of anyone, folks? - write and perform the Irish entry for that particular year?

Yes, the one where they sing: 'My Little Horse Running Through The Field'? You must remember that one, folks. I believe the vocals carried the lack of guitar work. 'My Little Horse Running Through The Field'? (Now try getting that out of your head for the rest of the day.)

I come downstairs and zero in on the fridge. It's like I am on auto-pilot. I fire a few jolts of Prosecco beyond my thrapple. And then a few more to keep those suds company.

In the meantime, there is still this wailing and hollering coming from the front room. I have no idea what I am about to confront. I have to think fast, so I turn back to the fridge and finish off the bottle. Seems like a reasonable plan, does it not?

Am I fortified enough to face today's insanity on offer from the husband/little drongo?

It is in moments like these that I believe you can separate those who do and those who say, dear friends. I open another bottle of bubbles and neck the lot in about thirty seconds. Now I am ready for the demons of lockdown day 170.

I push open the door to the front room. The miniscule pipsqueak has erected a sleeping bag, stuffed it with God only knows what, and it is now dangling precariously from the ceiling.

The little dweeb is dancing around it, throwing punches, of the powderpuff variety, at the suspended target.

Now I recognise the racket. It is 'Eye of the Tiger', that infernal ear-splitting offering from Survivor that was played incessantly in Rocky III. The power chords are reverberating around the room. There is no sign of Claude the cat. If the feline has any sense she'll be in Toronto by now.

'Hi, ma'am,' squeaks the little halfwit. 'I'm ... duh ... Rocky Balboa.'

A revolver never seems to be in the vicinity just when you need it most, is it, dear friends? I reckon a bullet between his beady eyes would bring an abrupt halt to this nonsense.

'Ah'm ... duh ... fighting for the ... duh ... world championship in ... duh ... half ... duh ... an hour,' he mumbles. As impressions of equally brain-dead Sylvester Stallone go, it wasn't too bad. (Mind you, the dopey actor picked up billions for the boxing movie that looked uncannily like 'Champion', with Kirk Douglas which was made about three decades earlier. Or any other fight film ever produced, when I come to think of it. So, possibly appearances can be deceiving as far as Rocky/Stallone is concerned.)

The little nitwit is still slapping his paws off the sleeping bag with featherlight effect. If I was a betting girl I would have my mortgage on the sleeping bag to win in the third round by a technical knock-out.

'I ... duh ... am ... gonna beat ... duh ... da bum,' he mutters. He is wearing an old Rolling Stones t-shirt with the gigantic tongue bursting through the equally massive lips. He has also located a pair of pink-and-white candy-striped shorts I'm sure used to be owned by Mrs Wilberforce before she switched to purple bloomers. He is also wearing his favourite pair of battered red wellingtons. It's not a good look.

I repair to the fridge for another bottle of the required medicinal suds. 'Eye of the Tiger' is still blaring out, ricocheting off every corner of the house, shaking dust from the rafters (perhaps I have neglected my cleaning duties these past few weeks . . . or years).

I am in dire need of inspiration, dear friends. And then I remember the words of the one-and-only Muhammad Ali. Remember his Rope-A-Dope tactics when he fought George Foreman?

I neck another bottle of Prosecco, repair to the back garden, fetch the clothes line, make a lasso and return to the front room.

Cowboy-like, I swirl the rope above my head before throwing it around the dancing midget and yank him off his feet. I make sure there is no sign of the vile Mrs Bottomley-Smythe or any of her bloodthirsty OAP crones hanging around the neighbourhood.

Then, I drag the village idiot into the street and I await my opportunity. I spy Mrs Wilkinson driving her Fiat Panda at her usual five-miles-per-hour as she heads out of the village. (Apparently a loaf of bread is one pence cheaper at Asda than it is at the village store and she will never overlook such a bargain.)

As she crawls past at snail's pace, I attach one end of the rope to her back fender (no laughing at the back, please) and wish the husband/ Rocky/little pillock goodbye and good luck.

I wave to him as he tries to remain upright. All I can hear is 'Ah've got a ... duh ... world championship ... duh ... fight in ... duh ... half ... duh ... an hour' as he disappears into the distance.

Now that is what I call boxing clever. With a bit of luck, I will have at least three hours to myself before Mrs Wilkinson passes on her way home.

I wonder how many bottles of Prosecco I can down in that stretch of time. I decide to put it to the test.

'Eye of the Tiger' is still thundering out as I thrust my hands into the air Ali-like and take the applause of the non-existent fans.

Hic! Hic! Hooray!

LOCKDOWN, day 172

Thursday, September 10

Today, I am a tad perturbed. I awake full of the joys, as usual, ready to combat the curve balls the world continues to throw in my direction. I stretch my aching limbs - the head is not too clever, either, if I'm being honest - and step over the discarded Andy Pandy pyjamas (don't ask).

You may have noticed, dear friends and fellow-sympathisers, the husband/little dumbbell is working his way steadily through his night-time attire during lockdown.

Thankfully, he has not yet indulged in Muffin The Mule (oh, please, Edina and you lot at the back, a bit of decorum, please).I slip into my favourite jumpsuit (not unlike the one Freddie Mercury used to prance excitedly and energetically around in during Queen concerts) and I head off on my Prosecco Pilgrimage. So far so good.

So, why am I a smidgen anxious this morning, I hear you ask? Possibly stressed out from the rigours of confronting lockdown day 172? Even the miniscule village idiot could work out that is almost twenty-five weeks. That's a lot of weeks. It's enough to turn you to strong ale if, of course, you had not already been on the slalom run of suds for the past decade or so.

Thank you for your concern, dear friends, but I am not running short of Prosecco (God forbid). The fridge, one of my favourite places on the planet, is well-stocked for another day on the lash and there is the emergency supply in the garage. (Some day, we'll find space for the car.) So, all is well on that front.

Actually, the problem is drink-related, but, thankfully, it has nothing to do with soaring prices of intoxicating bubbles. After all we are being forced to endure, that could be the bombshell news that tips us all over the edge.

The consternation comes from a newspaper headline. The little drongo has somehow manoeuvred his way across the road to the Village Store, skilfully bypassing the deeply objectionable Mrs Bottomley-Smythe, owner of the local tearoom, and her bunch of toxic crones who are still demanding retribution for some of his slightly more off-the-wall antics, including, of course, his penchant for nude roller skating.

Frankly, they are very fortunate they have yet to witness his naked limbo dancing. My Great Auntie Phoebe did not know where to look when the little dingbat (alas, little in every sense of the word, dear friends) performed the ritual one day just as tiffin was served. Funnily enough, she has never again darkened this household's doorstep and, in fact, has not returned a single phone call since that fateful afternoon. I wonder why?

Sorry, I appear to have lost the thread again. A few jolts of required Prosecco will no doubt help get me back on track. I get on the outside of a full bottle of breakfast and repair to the front room.

I note the dingbat has been shopping. He has remembered the Daily Bulletin and added a box of soap powder, a Radio Times from last month, an empty tube of smarties, and four hundred manila envelopes.

The headline in the newspaper hits me between the peepers. I race to the fridge for some much-needed fortification (I said fortification, you lot at the back. Edina, you are a bad influence. Watch your step.)

'ONE MILLION SCOTS HIT THE BOTTLE IN LOCKDOWN'.

My immediate concerns are for the four-and-a-half million who are missing out. The intro reads: One million Scots drinkers admit they have hit the booze harder during lockdown, raising fears of a health 'time bomb'.

Health time bomb? They think they have concerns with just a mere one million getting legless on a daily basis? How would they cope if the husband/little nonentity decided to attempt to indulge in what I have told him is 'adult juice'?

I mean, dear friends, we all know he is stone-cold bonkers 24/7 without the aid of an injection of alcohol, don't we? The brain-dead twerp hitting the bottle?

Now that's a sobering thought. Well, almost…

LOCKDOWN, day 176

Monday, September 14th

Today, I awake to what sounds like the onset of World War III.

I sit bolt upright in my pit and my peepers shoot open, the overnight gunge immediately being unlocked. It's just a pity the little dweeb who shares the marital bed is not around or I could have punched him in the face to make sure I wasn't dreaming.

There is thunderous crashing reaching ear-splitting levels. I can't even blame the miniscule drongo because the noise is erupting from all over the village.

I wondered for a moment if some of the dork's friends had come to visit, as some sort of convention for halfwits. Then I remember the pillock doesn't have any acquaintances.

Even Mrs Thorngood's toothless, veteran spaniel, Little Miss Gumsy, tries to take a bite out of the buffoon when he is allowed to roam the neighbourhood on the rare occasions he is not being feverishly pursued by the villainous Mrs Bottomley-Smythe, owner of the local tearoom, and her collection of bloody-thirsty OAP crones.

I am shaken from my delightful reverie of Miss Gumsy's gummy jaw clamped around the husband's behind by the continued crashing outside. I really need to get out of the scratcher to investigate what is creating such mayhem. Plus I urgently require some bottled breakfast.

I swing my feet onto the floor and almost step on his discarded Bob Monkhouse pyjamas (don't ask).

Without hesitation, I stagger in the direction of my rather packed wardrobe. You don't know this, dear friends, but I actually started a collection of old clothes for charity circa 1974 and now I have about twenty bin bags taking up valuable space in the wardrobe. (Memo to self:

Get your finger out, girl.) Still, I can't let my little walking nightmare have all the fun playing dress up and I do enjoy a good fumble in the morning (a fumble through my clothes, for goodness sake you lot at the back).

This morning, I struggle vainly with bundles of assorted garments. This must be what it is like for someone to attempt to hack their way through a dense forest. At last, I get a hold of my favourite Mama Cass jumpsuit (don't ask) and I quickly dress.

Gingerly, I move downstairs and wonder if I should investigate the cacophony that is engulfing the village. Maybe I should look in the kitchen just in case there are some Japanese soldiers roaming around because someone has forgotten to tell them the war is over.

Bravely, I take the kitchen route. Phew, dear friends! There are no Japanese soldiers in sight. I decide to celebrate my near escape with a bottle of Prosecco. It lasts just under fifty seconds.

Put yourself in my unfortunate position, please - my nerves are shot to pieces this morning, and for good reason! I can almost feel our ancient cottage reverberate with the racket from outside. What would you do? Yes, me, too. I decide to whip a second bottle out of the fridge and fire a few jolts behind my necktie. (Thank you for the advice, folks, I knew I could rely on you.)

Now slightly calmer, I make my way uncertainly across the hall. I have no idea what awaits me behind the door to the front room as I push it open and peak around the corner.

'Take cover, Cap'n Mainwairing!' shrieks the dingbat, cowering at the side of the sofa.

The waste of skin is in full battle dress with an upturned soup pan on his empty cranium. He is wearing flippers and clutching a rolled-up umbrella so hard his knuckles are white.

'It's war, Cap'n Mainwairing,' he screams. 'Can you hear the bombs? It's Armadillo, I tell you.'

I can't be bothered informing him there is no sign of a small creature with a leathery shell and sharp claws and possibly the word he is looking for is Armageddon.

'Good morning, nutter,' I offer as a substitute greeting.

There is still a riot of noise outside, and I make my way to the front window to see if, indeed, it is Armageddon. Dear friends, you'll be relieved to hear that it is only the council binmen. After a lockdown delay of several months, they have at last got around to emptying our purple bins. That is the colour designated for objects such as bottles, bottles and some more bottles. I realise at once that last week's newspaper was right: the village may have a slight drink problem with the amount of shattering, splintering and disintegrating glass that is now registering on the Richter Scale.

I have to confess I rather sneakily disposed of possibly a couple of hundred empty Prosecco containers from January onwards with a few midnight runs. Well, I didn't want to embarrass myself, did I? My purple bin was full a couple of days after it was emptied. I'm sure a jam jar pushed up the level.

'It's Armadillo, Cap'n Mainwairing,' repeats the little buffoon, quivering uncontrollably with the see-through umbrella I bought from Woolworths in 1964, his weapon of choice to fend off an Exocet Missile.

'Hold on,' I say, 'I'll get reinforcements.' I race back to the fridge and gurgle with the suds. Job done, I return to the front room.

'They're coming to get us, Cap'n Mainwairing,' he whines.

'I'll have a quick look out the window,' I say as I tiptoe past him as stealthily as I can.

'May I borrow your soup pan?' I ask.

'If you must, Cap'n Mainwairing,' he mutters weakly.

I remove the soup pan and, naturally, I administer a dull one to the unprotected napper. Whack! Bang on target and he's down.

I'm sorry, dear friends, I had to put him to sleep for a couple of hours. There is enough noise out there without him creating a din in here.

'Stupid boy, Pike,' I chide as I step over his prone body on my way back to the fridge.

I've got a purple bin to fill.

LOCKDOWN, day 177

Tuesday, September 15

Today, I am so excited. I have been reliably informed by the weather forecasters that we are about to celebrate our annual one day of summer.

We are not overly-exposed to that rare phenomenon of sunshine in this part of the universe, hence most of the inhabitants looking like extras from 'The Walking Dead'.'Pasty-faced,' I think is the term most used to describe the collection of Casper lookalikes who bumble around in desperate hope of that giant orange orb making its one-off appearance through the dark and foreboding clouds that dominate our modest corner of the planet.

I always have to remind the husband/little simpleton to cover up when the rays make their welcome presence Normally, I make him wear garments right up his neck. He spends the rest of the month with a bright red face and an alabaster white torso and legs. The little dweeb is quite thin, so he actually bears an uncanny resemblance to an elongated matchstick.

Lately, of course, he has discovered mankinis and what he looks like after being exposed to any sort of sunshine is anyone's guess. I would prefer not to dwell on this subject until I have been well fortified (oh, for goodness sake, Edina, and you lot at the back. I said 'well fortified'.)

I swing my sorry legs out of bed and climb over his Billy Dainty pyjamas (don't ask). I drag open the curtains and the sunshine blitzes my peepers. It's quite astonishing, dear friends and fellow-sympathisers. The weather forecasters have got it right. They can now go back to being hopelessly inaccurate for the remainder of the year. Their work is done for 2020.

Hurriedly, I throw myself into my Dame Edna Everage jump suit (don't ask) and head downstairs to the fridge for a small heart-starter. The presence of the sun hovering above the village calls for a mild celebration. (Not that I require a reason to pop a cork or two, as you well know by now, folks.)

I enjoy a few jolts of Prosecco and once again I am well impressed by the therapeutic qualities of the suds. I make sure the second bottle is at precisely the same temperature as the first and fire it behind my necktie. I reckon this a two-bottle breakfast sort of day. I make sure there is an array of substitutes on the bench and make my way through to the front room.

Once again, there is an ominous silence. The husband/little pipsqueak has not been reprimanded - as I like to term his regular whacks to his empty cranium - for a few days and I begin to wonder if he is okay.

He is sitting on the sofa in his best lilac Speedos (why am I not surprised?). I admit, he looks quite fetching in an imbecilic sort of way.

'Gerda,' he squeaks, 'the big red thing is in the sky.' The little drongo can hardly contain his excitement and normally that does not bode well. I know what I am talking about, dear friends. I am the one who has to clean up after the little pest.

'Yes, I have noticed, the husband,' I say and add: 'Would you like a barbecue today?'

He leaps from the sofa and begins bouncing up and down. In his enthusiasm, he has a bit of a wardrobe malfunction. I fear it will take some time before I can rid my memory bank of that image.

I repair to the kitchen for a little assistance. A few gurgles later, I return to the scene of the crime. He is still leaping around like Zebedee on speed.

'I take that is a 'yes', then, you little madman?' I say with a heavy hint of sarcasm that is noted by Claude the cat, but missed entirely by the semi-naked cavorting buffoon.

I scribble out a note of my requirements for the local butcher. The usual stuff - burgers, sausages, chicken and under-the-counter Prosecco.

I explain to the little halfwit he has to go to Mr Beef (not his real name, I hope) to pick up the supplies for the barbecue. Naturally, to ensure the drongo doesn't misplace it on his way to Mr Beef, I thoughtfully staple the shopping list to his right earlobe. (I have been assured he will not feel too much pain in this area.)

I have also glued an envelope with the cash to his right hand. What could possibly go wrong?

Actually, I don't particularly trust the butcher who appears to be bereft of a sense of humour.

After he had just opened his shop, I went along to buy some provisions to supplement the suds. I admit I was in a slightly mischievous mood, dear friends.

'Do you have pig's trotters?' I enquired.

'Yes, ma'am,' he replied.

'Well, I'll have a pound of mince, then, Porky.'

Didn't crack a smile. Always be wary of a man who cannot take a joke, folks.

I remind the little dumbbell to be on guard to the threat of the villainous Mrs Bottomley-Smythe, owner of the local tearoom, and her collection of odious OAPs who appear to be hell-bent on savaging the little twerp.

I tell him it might be good idea if he covers up the Speedos, which he does with his trusty raincoat and his kilt. He is also wearing his favourite red wellies and, as per usual, they are on the wrong feet. For absolutely no good reason, he is also wearing a snorkel. I say nothing. I just want him to get to Mr Beef, pick up the burgers etc (not forgetting the emergency bubbles) and get back here without mishap. Off he trundles, smothered in suntan lotion that is over twenty-five years old (naturally, we do not have much call for the cream, and I don't like to waste things).

I fire up the barbecue and, rather amazingly, the little cretin makes it back in one piece. I notice the snorkel has been mislaid and I shudder at the thought where it may have been misappropriated. I immediately have another couple of gurgles to soothe my nerves.

'Mr Beef said he has included a surprise,' trills the little nutter. He places the package on the table. Happily, I note two bottles of Prosecco have survived the journey Immediately, they are placed in the emergency rack.

I undo the wrapping. There are no burgers. No sausages. No chicken. Instead, dear friends, there is a huge slab of meat.

There is a note attached to it. 'Enjoy, Funny Lady.' It is signed Porky. I look at the mound of meat and I detect its origin.

Undeterred, I place it on the barbecue and sigh.

Altogether now, folks: 'Whale meat again, don't know where, don't know when, but I know whale meat again some sunny day.'

Good luck trying to get that song out of your head for the rest of the day.

(One more time: 'Whale meat again ...)

LOCKDOWN, day 178

Wednesday, September 16

Today, I awake feeling arty (no, that is not the name of a neighbour, you lot at the back. I realise it is difficult, but could you please behave?).

No, my dear friends and fellow-sympathisers, there are occasions where I feel this strange poetic surge firing through my being and I am left wondering if I missed my calling.

Surely, the Good Lord did not place me on this planet merely to look after a feeble-minded little chap who has the ability to irritate me on a daily basis? I feel I have a bit more to offer before I shuffle off this mortal coil.

Anyway, I feel those inspirational juices flowing - and for once I don't mean Prosecco - as I open my peepers and prepare to duel with the rigours of lockdown day 178. It begins well enough as I manage to miss stepping on his Honey Monster pyjamas (don't ask). Alas, this is as close to honey or a monster I am ever likely to encounter in the marital bed. C'est la vie, as they say in the art galleries of downtown Lille.

As I glide into my Frankie Vaughan jumpsuit (don't ask) I come over all a-tingle. (No, Edina and Co, it has nothing to do with withdrawal symptoms. Shame on you.)

So, here is my offering of verse:

As far as fame goes, they are hardly A-listers,

And they are certainly no friends of the mister's,

They leave you in no doubt of their craving for cake,

You can be sure they'll chomp and scoff all you can bake,

Yes, folks, please put your hands together for the Pidgeon Sisters.

That's right, we're having visitors for lunch today. That sounds a bit cannibalistic, doesn't it? Shall rephrase, dear friends. I will be entertaining two guests for luncheon. Actually, that's not quite right, either. I won't be entertaining them, I will be preparing sandwiches. Yes, I think that covers all bases.

You may remember the rather plumpish double-act of Layla and Lola who came over to our household a few weeks ago. It was a pleasant afternoon, though there was a slight kerfuffle with the miniscule halfwit who was well warned not to mention their lardy proportions. Of course, the little pillock put his foot in it and the Pidgeons swept as one to administer dull ones that I could only admire.

However, let bygones be bygones is my watchword and we will try once again to indulge in some social intercourse (oh, for goodness sake, you lot at the back).

I think I made it clear in my notes at the time that the Pidgeon sisters are no strangers to the dining table. Okay, they are of the well-upholstered variety. In fact, let me put it this way, dear friends: when they go on a continental holiday (remember them?) Britain raises two inches out of the water. This is only a slight exaggeration.

Anyway, I have taken the little dweeb aside to once again warn him of thinking before he opens his trap. I insist he must show a little decorum (oh for goodness sake, Edina.) He has been threatened with death - or something worse - if he does not behave.

The Pidgeons arrive around midday. Of course, I am well fortified courtesy of a couple bottles of Prosecco. As the sisters wedge their outsize buttocks into the sofa, I have a question for them which I hope does not offend.

In their hey-day - which wasn't last Thursday, I hasten to point out - Layla and Lola were known as L's Belles. (That's actually quite clever, isn't it?)

I wondered if they were a singing duet or, a stretch of the imagination, I accept, a dancing double-act.

So, while they devour a mountain of Battenberg and mumble incomprehensibly through the crumbs, I take the chance to ask my question.

Just as I'm about to put my query to the Pidgeons, the husband/little simpleton enters the front room.

'Were you a singing duet?' I ask. 'When you were L's Belles? Or, perhaps, dancers?'

'Fat chance,' squeaks the husband/little twerp.

Once again, the tubby twosome defy gravity as they spring from the sofa like ravenous cougars. The little dingbat does not stand a chance. Inside ten seconds he is pulverised to a pulp. The Pidgeons in full pelt are quite an awesome sight, folks.

The little dumbbell will be out for at least two hours, I reckon. The Pigeons chorus: 'We have never been so insulted.'

'You should get out more,' I mutter.

As they prepare to leave in an indignant huff - swiping the last of the jelly and sponge cake as they go - I have to get an answer.'Why were you called L's Belles?' I ask again.

'Didn't you know, dear?' smiles Layla.

'We were tag-team wrestlers,' says Lola.

I bite my tongue. How big were the wrestling rings back then? When they were in the building, where did they fit the audience? Some questions are best unasked. I allow them to barge their way through the front door on their way out.

I step over the wrecked body of the little pipsqueak on my way to the fridge and another visitation with the bubbles.

LOCKDOWN, day 180

Friday, September 18

Today, the husband is required to go for a much-needed haircut. For some obscure reason lost on me, the little dweeb does not want me anywhere near him with sharp implements.

I did make the pitch that the drongo could save a couple of shekels which, of course, I would put to a good use ie the Prosecco Fund, if I were to take the scissors to his rather wayward barnet. (Memo to self: If lockdown continues for much longer, buy a bigger fridge.)

He looks like a gonk - remember them? - that has trod on a live electric wire. And remember Ken Dodd with his tickling stick? He is a ringer for the tickling stick.

Anyway, the miniscule pipsqueak now believes it is time for a visit to barbers. This is not the worst idea he has ever had in his miserable existence, though to be fair, it doesn't have much competition. I am not complaining, but I have not seen his ears since the end of March and I am thoroughly fed up with the TV volume at full blast and the constant chattering of: 'What did she say?' 'Eh?' 'What did he say?' 'Whit?' 'What's going on?'.

Conversations with the little moron are rarely noteworthy, but they are reaching new levels of mundane.

Once again, dear friends and fellow-sympathisers, is it any wonder I thank Mr and Mrs Prosecco and all the little Proseccos every day?

So, once again, I allow my peepers to get used to the daylight before I swing my legs out of the marital bed and step over his discarded Rod Stewart pyjamas (don't ask).

I put on my favourite Winnie The Pooh jumpsuit (don't ask) as one wants to look presentable for public appearances, doesn't one? I have even removed the hair curlers for the occasion. (From my head, not the Winnie The Pooh jumpsuit.)

The barbers don't open until 9am and I have made an extra special effort to remove my carcass from its slumber position quite early to make sure everything is in place for the numbskull to get to the hairdressers. Frankly, I still believe I could do the job fairly well with the lawn mower, but he is steadfastly against this suggestion. The little madman has no sense of adventure.

The upside, of course, of being on my toes so early is that breakfast can also kick off quicker than normal. There is a God, dear friends.

I fire a few jolts of bubbles behind my necktie and have to admit it is quite a pleasant sensation at this unknown hour of the day. (Memo to self: Suds are a worthy substitute for sleep.) I then head for the front room where I prepare to meet the Wild Man of Borneo. Actually, it's not that bad, but he does look like a refugee from The Rolling Stones.

'Good morning, nutter,' I say by way of a pleasant greeting.

He says nothing. I can see he is quite nervous. He has reasoned that he should wear his best mauve mankini for the visit to the hair salon. Go figure.

Anyway, I drive him to the local barbers - only clipping a few fire hydrants and having a near miss with Mr Barlow on the way - and he is helped to his chair. I remind him the nice man is a hairdresser and not a dentist. He appears to be reassured by my words, the little fool.

The barber gets to work immediately, clipping away merrily. He asks all the usual questions hairdressers do to while away the hours. 'Still knocking about with Pixie Lott? Robbed any good banks recently? Still living on the moon? Do penguins have knees? Do hens smile?' That sort of thing.

The dork sits there quietly as his helmet of hair is trimmed down . So far nothing has gone even slightly awry, dear friends. And then it happens.

The hairdresser looks the other way for just a moment. Somehow, the little buffoon gets his tongue caught in his clippers. Apparently, he mistook them for a lolly. As he starts to lick them, the halfwit hits the 'on' switch.

I have never heard screams like it. The walls shook as he shrieked and yelled.The hairdresser almost passed out with anxiety as the doofus bounced around the salon. What to do, dear friends? Luckily I had secreted a bottle of Prosecco upon my person. You never know when you might get caught in a snowdrift.

As the little dumbbell gyrates around the room - not unlike Mick Jagger on one of his better days, I must confess - I drain the contents. Well, I wasn't going to hit him with a full bottle, was I? Take the chance of some spillage? No chance.

I administer a dull one mid-chant and down goes the pillock. All is quiet as I help him to his feet and drag him by his heels to the car.

I receive some funny looks from passers-by.

'He's just had his hair cut,' I say by way of explanation.

LOCKDOWN, day 181

Saturday, September 19

Today, I awake (thank the Good Lord for that) and topple out of bed.

I prepare for yet another infernal week in lockdown. Can you believe that, dear friends and sympathisers, almost TWENTY-SIX weeks?

Still half asleep at this ridiculously early hour of just before noon, I stumble over the little drongo's Bing Crosby pyjamas (don't ask).

Bleary-eyed, with my usual trepidation – and a slightly sore head (admittedly Prosecco-induced) – I wander downstairs. All is quiet. Where is the village idiot who doubles as what is laughingly known as the husband?

My instincts lead me to the fridge (no surprise there, I suppose) to have a small sip of refreshing crisp, cold spring water. Who am I kidding? I go straight for the bubbles and shake loose a few mouthfuls. And then another few. Suddenly, the bottle is empty. I make sure there is another sentry on duty. Thankfully, there is and it is with a fair amount of satisfaction and pleasure that I note there is a whole regiment behind him. They don't stand a chance. I have a small drouth today.

Fortified, I toddle towards the front room. What fresh madness lies therein? I push open the door.

The little dweeb is sitting on the sofa in his best chef whites. I think I have been in this movie before. The halfwit has obviously watched one of those annoying cookery programmes on TV and in his empty head he believes he is Gordon Ramsay Mark Two. (Personally, I believe we have enough problems with foul-mouthed Gordon Ramsay Mark One.)

I look at the miniscule pillock as he sits there with a large wooden fork in one hand and a large wooden spoon in another. (Jeezo, what turmoil is around the corner this fine Saturday?)

137

'Good morning, my little recurring pain in the rectum,' I say by way of a greeting.

'Good afternoon,' he corrects me in his irritating little squeak. (He is already on thin ice and I haven't even got on the outside of my second bottle of Prosecco.)

'Why are you dressed like Casper?' I ask.

'Casper who?' he asks.

'Casper the friendly ghost,' I answer.

'I don't believe in ghosts,' he says blithely.

I feel my will to live quickly leaving my body.

'Do you believe in flying saucers?' I ask.

'No,' he smirks.

I whip a saucer off the table and scud it off the top of his head.

'You do now. What's with the white gear?'

'I think we'll have a barbecue today, my little sausage roll,' he says, rubbing vigorously at the top of his cranium.

It is quite a nice day in in this part of the universe. (Bring out the bunting, let's have a street party, make the most of it while we can.) A barbecue also means I don't have to cook. A win-win (more Prosecco) situation for me.

The twenty five year old suntan lotion is depleted, so, once he has disrobed from his Casper/Gordon Ramsay disguise to head for the back garden, I smother him in olive oil. (Well, it seemed a good idea at the time and it had been on special at the local supermarket. I've got rivers of the stuff.)

I tell him it is for his own protection. I also explain it would be a good idea if he protected his head from the elements, although, really, why bother? It's not like there are any brains in there to scramble, are there?

He races off to his Aladdin's Cave at the back of the house, the area where no right-minded person would dare enter, and comes back adorned with his Noddy hat. He is now wearing a pair of Martina Navratilova-endorsed tennis shorts that are about ten sizes too big for him. To keep them in place, he has attached red and rather large braces, much favoured by circus clowns.

He has decided to go with his Bruce Willis 'Die Hard' vest and his favourite scuffed sandals. And, naturally, his Andy Pandy and Big Ears novelty socks his Great Aunt Philomena gave him for his fifth birthday. (She didn't like him much.) Andy, as usual, is on the left and Big Ears on the right. Overall, he has worn more outrageous outfits, as you could testify, dear friends, but it's still not a good look.

The dunce eventually divests himself of his 'Die Hard' vest as he sets the coals alight without, miraculously, setting fire to the entire village.

After an hour or so, he remembers to put on the burgers. You should see his happy little face. He is so eager to please after his recent misdeeds and mishaps. However, his smile soon falls and he begins to sweat profusely. His face turns the most awful colour of magenta. Soon, blisters pop up on the back of his neck.

'Gerda, my sweetness and light,' he gasps, 'I think I am burning up.'

And with that he collapses backwards, smashing his Noddy head off the largest rock in the rock garden. I think the barbecue may be cancelled.

As he lies in a crumpled heap, I repair to the fridge for much-needed fortification. The suds help soothe my fevered brow with every cascade beyond my thrapple. After another two bottles, I note the little nutter has not moved from his prone position amid the rocks.

With the local A&E on speed dial, I notify them they are about to receive a visit from their favourite client/customer/dork.

Edith and Morgan are ecstatic to see him. They haven't seen him for a couple of weeks and they were beginning to worry if something had happened to the little dweeb.

They look at the sizzling offering in front of them - with a large bump beginning to form on the back of his napper - and chorus: 'What on earth happened this time, Gerda?'

I tell them about splashing him with gallons of olive oil and the sun beating down on him incessantly.

How we laughed when they told me of the consequences of such an action.

It could have been worse, dear friends. I could have put some olive oil on myself. Thankfully, I utilised the remains of the suntan lotion.

LOCKDOWN, day 182

Sunday, September 20

Today, I awake in a reasonably good mood which, naturally, is excellent news for the little dweeb who shares the marital bed. Twenty-four hours could pass without the administration of a dull one. Though I make no promises.

I have been asked about my treatment of the village idiot and I believe some think it is a tad harsh. All I can say, dear friends and fellow-sympathisers, it pains me, too, when I feel the need to bring swift and urgent retribution to proceedings.

Just the other day I almost staved my thumb. I wasn't holding the neck of the bottle of Prosecco properly (empty, of course) when I swung it as his vacuum-filled cranium. It really jarred, I can tell you. I had to neck an entire bottle of bubbles to dull the ache.

And don't worry about the drongo. He regained consciousness about two hours later. Alas, it was not one of my better efforts.

Back to today, though. My peepers adjust to late morning daylight as I swing my legs out of bed and narrowly miss stepping on his Leslie Phillips pyjamas (don't ask). Do you remember Leslie Phillips, the cad who used to pop up in all those old black and white movies (well before my time, naturally)? I recall he was famous for saying 'Ding dong' every five minutes in every film.

A statuesque blonde would teeter past on her skyscraper heels and he would twirl his moustache and say those immortal lines; 'Ding dong'. Everyone in the theatre would laugh.

Asked about the possible outbreak of war, Phillips would answer: 'Ding dong'. And everyone in the theatre would laugh.

It must have taken him about five minutes to learn his lines for each film. Now that's a job I could do. Possibly with a screen break for a few jolts of Prosecco in between 'ding' and 'dong'.

Anyway, dear friends, I slide into my George of the Jungle jumpsuit (don't ask) and head immediately for the fridge. My friends at Prosecco have been calling my name since my peepers became unglued.

Just to make certain I have not lost my edge, I get on the outside of a full bottle, those flowing contents hitting the mark in Happy Valley. Fortified, I head for the front room to see if the little pipsqueak is still the possessor of a pulse.

The husband is sitting on the sofa and, remarkably, he is not dressed as Elvis, Batman, Donald Trump or even Benny Hill. He actually looks almost normal. I said almost.

'Good morning, nutter,' I say by means of a greeting.

'Pfffft,' he replies.

'Sorry,' I say, 'I didn't catch that.'

'Pfffft,' he repeats.

By all standards, dear friends, this is an unusual retort even for someone who has been brain-dead since birth. I am well aware of his lack of skills in the communication department, but surely he can do better than this? I try once again to get the day off to a reasonable start.

'Good morning, nutter,' I repeat.

'Pffft,' he returns.

I am resisting the temptation to fire a few jolts behind my necktie and put the empty bottle to a good use.

'Have you now taken to speaking in some strange dialect unknown to man, you little waste of skin?' I ask, somewhat tersely.

'Pfffft,' he repeats.

I fear this may be a long day. I step closer to look at the little twerp (it's not exactly a feast for the orbs, I have to admit).

'Pfffft,' he says.

That's when I notice his mouth appears to be stuffed with paper. What fresh hell is this, I muse?

As gently as I can, I grab hold of his jaws and begin shaking furiously.

'Pffft ... pffft ... cough ... cough,' he responds.

Chunks of shredded newsprint erupt from his cakehole. Bits of paper flutter around the front room. Claude the cat thinks it's some sort of ticker-tape procession and walks proudly across the floor.

'Okay,' I say, 'there must be some sort of reasonable explanation.' (Though that would be a first, I think.)

'You saved my life, oh thank you, the brightest light in the history of brightness, the most radiant of all strawberry tarts,' he splutters.

'Never mind that guff, halfwit,' I say. (There is a time and place for romance, dear friends, and this was not it, especially not with bits of chewed-up newspaper stuck to the buffoon's nose.)

'I ate eight pages of the newspaper,' he wheezes.

I await a further explanation, I'm pretty certain there must be a reason even the dullard would stick his gnashers into the Daily Blah.

Silence.

'Why?' I ask and I cannot halt a trace of pleading in my tremor. 'Why would you do such a thing, you little dork?'

'It said so in the paper,' he replies and picks up the front page of the journal.

He points to the words across the top of the local rag. It reads: INSIDE! DELICIOUS EIGHT-PAGE RECIPE PULL-OUT. There really isn't enough time in the world for me to attempt to inform him the eight pages are of recipes for someone (not me) to arrange and cook for a real meal. The eight pages are not actually a meal in themselves.

I am saved the bother of having to repair to the fridge to pick up some ammo to administer a well-deserved dull one. I note his face is turning a rather strange colour of puce. He races off to the loo and I hear the melodic sounds of some feverish retching. I doubt if I will be bothered with his stupidity for at least another hour or so as he keeps the bowl company.

Ding dong.

LOCKDOWN, day 183

Monday, September 21

Today, I awake up slightly worse for wear. Someone let the cat out of the bag and alerted me to the fact that it was national Prosecco Day yesterday. I couldn't let the Prosecco family down, could I? As I recall through the haze of alcohol, I toasted the sudsy geniuses several times. And, just to show this was not a mere one-off show of affection for their invention, I fully intend to keep the celebrations going today. It's the least a gal can do. I think it is only right and proper I show my total and overwhelming appreciation by getting out of my face once more.

My peepers become unstuck as another day in hell beckons. For a moment, I wonder if I have been hit by a wrecking ball during my slumbers.

Gingerly, I edge my legs out of bed, making sure my head does not roll off at the same time. I step over his discarded Joanna Lumley pyjamas (don't ask).

I step into my sequined Elizabeth Taylor jumpsuit (don't ask) and struggle to pull up the zip. I have to confess, dear friends I may have put on a couple of pounds since lockdown began. (Memo to self: Put less water in tea.)

I head downstairs for the sanctuary that is the kitchen where my most prized asset, the fridge, resides quietly in the corner. I swish open the door, grasp a welcoming cold bottle of bubbly and bring it to my lips.

A couple of gurgles later and the world of Prosecco is down one of its number. Just to keep it company, I get on the outside of the contents of the second soldier. Those suds did not die in vain, dear friends.

Fortified, I drag myself in the general direction of the front room and wonder what awaits on this 183rd day of lockdown as I push open the door.

The dullard is standing in the middle of the room. My immediate thought is that the nutter has finally taken complete leave of what meagre senses he once possessed.

He has found a mop head, dipped it in something dark (where would he find all that treacle, I mused) and planted it on top of his empty cranium.

I note he has been in my wardrobe to borrow the fur coat I keep for weddings and funerals (alas, more of the latter these days, dear friends, as time continues to take no prisoners) and he has cut off the sleeves.

For some obscure reason, the pillock has found a deckchair and cut up the material, wrapped them around his puny legs and stuck them together with Sellotape. He thinks he has designed a pair of trousers. I also note he has found my old medallion I won at school for taking top prize in the egg and spoon race. (Yes, I cheated. a dollop of chewing gum applied to the shell worked wonders.) He has wrapped the massive piece of worthless tin on a chain and it is now dangling in front of his scrawny chest. It's not a good look.

'Okay, what's this all about, you little simpleton?' I ask. I admit my late-morning greeting may lack some genteel warmth.

'I got you, babe,' he squeaks.

'Unfortunately.' I shoot back.

'They say we're young and we don't know,' he mutters.

I say nothing.

'We won't find out until we grow ... '

Silence.

'Well, I don't know if all that's true ... '

More silence.

'Cause you got me and, baby, I got you.'

I gaze at this freak show performing in front of me. The buffoon believes he is Sony Bono. That must make me Cher.

'I got you, babe,' he squeaks and gyrates his hips in a bizarre circular motion that looks as though a voyage to the nearest loo is an urgent requirement.

To be honest, dear friends, there are days - few and far between, I hasten to add - when I find the miniscule pipsqueak quite entertaining.

145

This is not one of those days.

'I got you, babe,' he whines again.

'Hold on,' I say as I repair to the fridge to neck a full bottle of Prosecco.

'Those aren't the words,' he squeals in protest. 'They say we're young and we don't know ... '

I return fully armed with an empty bottle.

'We won't find out until we grow ... '

I manoeuvre myself into a good position just to his left as he continues his rendition of the Top of the Pops circa 1965.

'Well, I don't know if that is true ... '

I swing the bottle, aiming at a strategic and vulnerable opening in the mop head. Smack and down goes the husband/Sony Bono/little twerp.

'I got you, babe,' I sing with a smile.

LOCKDOWN, day 189

Sunday, September 27

Today, I awake with a smile on my face. I can't stop thinking of a fond memory of last night. (No, none of that romantic malarkey, you lot at the back.)

I was in an extraordinarily good mood when I asked the little dweeb if he wanted a late supper. You should have seen his little face, dear friends and fellow-sympathisers. He practically leapt out of the sofa as he gleefully capped his hands and grinned his irritating little grin.

I asked him what he would like.

He said: 'Surprise me.'

So, I smacked him in the face with a right-hander.

Oh, how I laughed as he toppled over the back of the chair and lay prone for a good hour while I got on the outside of a couple of welcoming bottles of Prosecco. Yes, I know, my actions may have veered on the cruel side, but I could not resist.

So, before my peepers become unstuck to usher in another day in hell, I have a smile on my fizzog. The village idiot who shares the marital bed is nowhere to be seen, so presumably he is elsewhere making a nuisance of himself, probably having a full-blown conversation with the vase he believes is a parrot.

I swing my legs out of the pit and neatly sidestep his discarded Gene Hackman pyjamas (don't ask) as I make my way to the wardrobe to fish out something special for lockdown day 189. I settle on my Charles Hawtrey jumpsuit (don't ask) and head instinctively for the fridge. Suds await my urgent presence and I do not want to let them down.

I fire a few jolts behind my necktie and decide to denude the bottle of its entire contents. Satisfied, I do something similar with the second

147

bottle. Well, I say similar, but I mean identical. That sucker went off to Happy Valley in a trice.

Fortified, I make my way across the hall for the front room. What has the miniscule drongo to offer today, I wonder? What insanity awaits behind that door? I push it open and, yes, he has not disappointed yet again.

For reasons known only to himself, he is wearing a massive pair of black-rimmed spectacles. Thankfully, he has also adorned his puny frame with a fawn-coloured raincoat.

'Good morning, nutter,' I say by way of a late-morning greeting.

'You were only supposed to blow the bloody doors off,' he squeaks in some sort of bizarre Cockney accent.

'Pardon, halfwit?' I ask.

'The best research for playing a drunk is being a British actor for twenty years.'

I am struck dumb. What fresh madness is this?

'I see myself as 38, but you don't notice it.'

Silence.

'Obsession is a young man's game and my only excuse is that I never grew old.'

More silence.

''You get paid the same for a bad film as you do for a good one.'

I am seriously considering getting those nice people with self-hugging cardigans on speed dial at this point. It seems the husband may need a nice padded room and some sedatives.

'My most useful acting tip came from my pal John Wayne. Talk low and talk slow and don't say too much.'

The penny drops, dear friends.

'Are you, by any chance, Michael Caine?' I ask.

'Not a lot of people know that,' he mutters in some strange strangled tones.

'Are you the gentleman who was in Alfie? Zulu? The Italian Job?' I ask.

'Don't forget Get Carter,' he adds.

'Is that the movie where Michael Caine gets shot and is last seen lying on a beach with a bullet hole between his eyes?'

The dunce looks a little perplexed.

And so he should be. I see my opening. I repair to the fridge to neck a third bottle of bubbles. And you will have a fair idea how I will utilise the empty bottle, haven't you?

I return to the front room.

'You're a big man, but you're in bad shape. With me, it's a full-time job. Now behave yourself.'

I'm sorry, dear friends, but my compulsion to deliver a dull one is too demanding.

Plus I don't think I could be bothered with the dullard firing Michael Caine quotes at me all Sunday. Thwack! And down goes the husband/Alfie/Carter/little buffoon in a heap.

That's what he gets for making a spectacle of himself.

Boom! Boom!

LOCKDOWN, day 191

Tuesday, September 29

Today, I awake with a little trepidation. No, that's not a new name for the dweeb. I do have other monikers for the person who shares the marital bed, but it is not my intention to colour the air blue so early in the late-morning.

No, the reason for my trepidation is that we have a 'His 'n' Hers' visit to the dentist booked this afternoon. I have to lead the terrified drongo by the hand for his appointment with 'the nasty man in the white coat and the big screwdriver'.

The village idiot was never that frightened of the molar-pulling chap until he watched 'Marathon Man' one night with me. Do you remember the one, dear friends and fellow-sympathisers, where Laurence Olivier, as a nasty Nazi, has the nice Dustin Hoffman strapped down in the chair and is menacing him with a drill?

He says: 'Is it safe?'

And a terrified Dustin mumbles: 'Pfffft ... farffle ... dipple ... '

Olivier lifts the screeching dental equipment once more and lets it rotate under Dustin's nose.

'Is it safe?' he asks again.

'Pfffft ... farflle ... dipple ... ' replies a terrified Dustin.

This goes on for about half-an-hour, but, of course, the little drongo only witnessed about two minutes before passing out. Slumped on the floor for the remainder of the movie, I had to step over him about five times to help myself to a few jolts of Prosecco. Just to steady my nerves, you understand.

So, any time I mention to the dunce that it is time to visit the dentist - and I have to admit Dolly Simpkins DDS does bear an uncanny resemblance to Laurence Olivier at his molar-excavating meanest - the husband feigns death.

He collapses to the floor and squeaks: 'I can't go ... I have passed away ... I am an ex-person ... I am no longer on this planet.'

Normally, I allow this to go for about an hour before I give him a gentle nudge in the nether regions with a stiletto heel. That always has the desired effect, dear friends.

So, that is what I face today as my peepers become unstuck and another day in Dante's Inferno beckons. Prosecco, of course, will help me through.

I sweep my feet out of the scratcher and make sure I do not step on his discarded Alf Garnet pyjamas (don't ask) as I make my way to my wardrobe for today's selection. I rifle among the cobwebs and get my hands on my favourite Jimmy Durante jumpsuit (don't ask).

After a few jolts of bubbles which brings much-needed fortification (how many times do I have to tell you folk at the back?), I am just passing the telephone in the hallway when it shrills to life. After the short call I replace the receiver on the cradle and continue towards the door to the front room. What lies within, I wonder?

The dumbbell does not disappoint.

He is lying prone smack in the middle of the floor. He looks like a reject from The Mummy's Tomb. He has swathed himself in bed sheets and curtains and is flat out.

'Good morning, nutter,' I say by way of some sort of cordial greeting.

'Pffft ... farffle ... .dipple ... ' comes the response.

I am quite impressed he has memorised Dustin Hoffman's speech from The Marathon Man.

'Oh, I see, my little brain-dead friend, you are not looking forward to our meeting with Dolly Simpkins DDS?'

'Pfffft ... farffle ... dipple ... ' he repeats.

'Has rigor mortis set in yet, my little waste of oxygen?' I ask helpfully.

'Pffft ... farffle ... dipple,' he responds.

There is nothing else for it, dear friends. I repair to the kitchen and neck a full bottle of suds. I look out three ice buckets, carefully place a bottle in each container and wheel them through to the front room. I take my place in front of the TV and decide to watch a rerun of The Marathon Man.

All the way through I nudge the dork with my foot just to make sure he has not really passed away.

'Pffft ... farffle ... dipple ... ' he says on each occasion.

I put my feet on his face for comfort as I settle down for the day. This can go on for at least two hours, I reckon. Peace and quiet apart from the odd 'pffft ... farffle ... dipple.'

The telephone call? Oh, that was the dentist's receptionist letting me know they would have to cancel today's appointment. They'll see us next week. (If they're lucky.)

LOCKDOWN, day 196

Sunday, October 4

Today is a yay day. I awake and I say: 'Yay!' I don't say 'yay' every day. Not even in May do I say 'yay' every day although I may say 'yay' on a day even when the skies are grey and stay that way for the rest of the day. I may say hooray on another day that's not so grey.

My head is beginning to hurt. It must have been the eighth bottle of Prosecco. Or could it have been the ninth? Did I go into double figures in my pursuit of bubbles? I can't remember. Now where was I, dear friends and fellow-sympathisers?

Oh, yes, I awake with that rarest of phenomenon's - a smile on my face. I say 'yay'. (Editor's note: Don't start all that nonsense again.)

The smile, dear friends. is because I am on holiday. That's right, a couple of days ago, I jumped aboard a ferry (yes, I know, some people don't believe in ferries) and travelled across the River Clyde to a small Scottish island called Cumbrae. Being the astute gal I am - although I did let my guard down when I allowed the dweeb to take me up the aisle (oh, Edina, not again!) - I made sure to phone ahead and ensured the local supermarket was well stocked with Prosecco. They informed me they had gallons of the stuff. I told them they would need more than that. A lot more. I intended to make this a memorable break. Well, I probably won't be able to remember too much, if you catch my drift, dear friends.

Oh, I should mention, the doofus is on holiday with me. Yes I know, it is a shame I should be plagued by him even in this distant, foreign land, but he's behaved quite well so far. He looked out his bucket and spade in preparation and didn't change out of his beachwear and straw boater for several days before we left. I am not complaining, dear friends. I saw him looking lovingly at his brand new magenta mankini and I feared the worst.

The little island might be prepared to tolerate his stripey one-piece Victorian beach outfit, but I reckon they might have followed the lead of the odious Mrs Bottomley-Smythe, her vile bunch of OAP village vigilantes and the increasingly-annoying Mrs Wilberforce, and begin to throw rocks and out-of-date buns at the dork if he turned up wearing a mankini. Cumbrae is not ready for such garb, dear friends.

I do recall a few years ago, the miniscule cretin thought he would go naked roller gliding along the promenade. I managed to purchase some candy floss and place it strategically upon his person before anyone noticed his wardrobe malfunction - or rather, lack of wardrobe. Alas, it didn't take an awful lot of the puffed-up confectionery to cover his ... erm ... modesty.

I digress, dear friends. I am having fun on our holiday so far, though perhaps that's due to the fact the dork went missing for a day or so. When we first arrived on the island, I informed him of a shop at the top of a mountain that was giving away free Roy Rogers cowboy kits. You should have seen his little face when I imparted this gem of knowledge upon him.

He looked out his Elvis Presley Vegas outfit and his hiking boots and took off in the general direction of where I told him the shop was located. Poor wee soul was devastated when he returned a couple of days later and informed me he could not find the Roy Rogers emporium.

'I am so sorry, oh sweetness and light,' he muttered. 'I looked everywhere, even up some trees, but I could not discover where the shop was located. I feel I have let you down.'

He looked so wretched after trekking around in the wilderness with only a bottle of lemonade, a couple packets of cheese and onion crisps, and a Mars bar for sustenance. My heart went out to the fool.

'You know, you little waste of skin, I've just been told there's a shop selling Tarzan loincloths, just over there,' and I pointed vaguely off to the distance. The dingbat's face immediately lit up and off he trekked again, grabbing another Mars bar for the road.

That was two days ago, dear friends. I confess to you, there was never any Roy Rogers shop, nor one selling Tarzan loincloths. I just needed a little space from the dimwit - and who can blame me?

Anyway, there's no need to worry about the dweeb. Like the proverbial bad penny, he will return, hopefully in time to catch the ferry home, where I will resist all urges to shove him overboard.

But I have to reveal it is a tempting thought. I'll ponder my options while I crack open my next bottle of Prosecco.

LOCKDOWN, day 200

Thursday, October 8

Today, I awake to day 200 of the lockdown. It has been a hard slog to reach this milestone and yet again I offer my thanks to Mr and Mrs Prosecco and all the little Proseccos who have helped me on my tedious journey.

As you know, dear friends and fellow-sympathisers, the trip through hell has not been made any the easier by the dweeb with whom I share a marital bed. To make matters worse, the husband seems to have gone through transformation of sorts these past few days.

Perhaps it was the latest whack over his head with an empty Prosecco bottle that triggered this personality change, but the dimwit has turned into a mean, murderous, foul-mouthed Humphrey Bogart type of character. He has told me, more than once, that he's not adverse to 'plugging dumb broads full of holes' at the drop of a fedora.

I admit I live in fear. The husband/Bogart/drongo informs me he has a rod and he knows how to use it (oh, for goodness sake, you lot at the back, we're discussing life and death here).

This might shock you, dear friends, but I believe him. I look into those menacing, dark eyes, see that thin, wolfish grin, and I know the doofus aka Humphrey Bogart wouldn't give a plugged nickel if he had to ventilate my forehead. If only I knew what exactly caused this sudden metamorphosis from bumbling idiot to blood-thirsty gangster. All I know is that the nincompoop was hauled off by PC McIvor for questioning over some recent incidents the other day. Apparently, there had been multiple sightings throughout the village of a man rummaging through peoples' bins. Now, the pillock was only looking for supplies for some avant-garde art project (move over, Andy Warhol) but the police were none too pleased and kept him locked in a cell for a night. A night away from the drongo, I hear you say, sounds like heaven. You would think, dear friends,

156

but it's when he returned from his night in jail that the village idiot was no longer my beloved dingbat and was instead a fedora-wearing killer.

I wonder what lies in store for me today as I place my tooties on the bedroom floor and make my way silently to the fridge downstairs. I have no intention of upsetting the gat-toting (whatever that is) character and having the cottage redecorated in an explosion of claret. To assist me through this particular episode in one of Dante's Circles of Hell, however, I need Prosecco. I swing open the fridge door and my progress is halted.

'Bourbon. On the rocks. Tall glass. Now - If you know what's good for you, sister.' It is a coarse, harsh order barked from He Who Must Be Obeyed. He is even intruding into my bottled breakfast sojourn. How much of this can a gal take?

'Don't even think about lifting that damn bottle of bubbles to your lips, sweet cheeks. Bourbon. On the rocks. Tall glass. Now - if you know what's good for you.'

I do not wish to be blown away in a fusillade of bullets, so I do as I am ordered. I feel faint. The Prosecco is looking back at me, it is singing my name, the sweetest of lullabies, but I am aware I could be fitted for a Chicago overcoat at any time, so I dutifully pour the bourbon, making sure there is the correct quantity of ice and I use his favourite tall glass.

I take it through the front room. He is standing with one foot on the sofa, still wearing the fedora and trench coat.

'What kept you, peaches?' he snarls, a cigarette dangling loosely from his lower lip. He snatches the glass from me and sips the contents. 'Maybe too much frozen E20, sister, but I'll let it slide this time. Do it again and you'll be in a whole heap of trouble. Capiche?' He sneers at me as I quiver in front of him.

'I capiche,' I say and withdraw as swiftly as I can to the kitchen. Two bottles of suds find their way to Happy Valley in double-quick time. I reckon it is a personal best. Actually, it's probably a world record.

I return to the front room only moderately fortified (sorry for letting you down, Edina) and I wonder what is next on my agenda of misery. At this point the doorbell rings. The husband/Bogart/halfwit immediately straightens up and thrusts his right hand inside his coat. I reckon he's going for his equaliser.

'See who it is, Doris,' he barks. 'Any funny stuff and Jonathan T

Blunderbus will start coughing. Capiche? Edgar J Firefly ain't going back to no slammer. It's them or us, baby.'

I make my way to the front door and somewhat surprised to be confronted by PC McIvor. I wonder what this Satan in a cop's uniform has in store for yours truly.

'Ma'am, I think I might owe you an apology,' he says and he does look a tad contrite. Life is full of surprises these days.

'You remember we requested your husband assist us with some enquiries the other day?' PC McIvor is shifting back and forth on his feet like a naughty school boy. I say nothing. 'Well, to be honest, we wondered if maybe your husband was under the influence of hallucinogenic drugs at the time. We asked him a few questions, but we couldn't get much sense out of him.'

Nothing unusual there, at least not for the doofus.

'And we decided to keep him in the night for his own safety. I hope you agree this was the right thing to do?'

I say nothing.

'Well, some of the ladies in town say that your husband has been especially aggressive towards them recently. We've had reports from Mrs Bottomley-Smythe and Mrs Wilberforce that he threw rock-hard buns and stale cakes at them the other day.'

'I think you could say he was returning the confectionery that was chucked at him in the first place,' I say.

'Oh, yes, a little fun and frolics with the ladies of the neighbourhood,' he says, but doesn't smile. 'Possibly all a little misunderstanding.' He looks at me. I stare back. Where is he going with this inane babble?

'This is quite a change in character for your husband, wouldn't you agree ma'am? I mean, he's always been a smidgen on the puny side, if you don't mind me making the observation. So, I got to thinking about why he would attack Mrs Bottomley-Smythe and her lady companions all of a sudden. And then I remembered we put him in a cell the other night with Harry The Hippo.'

'Harry The Hippo?' I ask and I wonder if I should punch myself in the face to make sure I am not having another horrible dream.

'Well, he's a guy who calls himself Harry The Hippo. Actually, he's a bit of a hypnotist. Not bad, apparently, when he's sober, and that's probably why we throw him in the cells quite a lot. To help him sober up, if you know what I mean?'

'Harry The Hippo?' I repeat.

'Oh, yes,' says PC McIvor. 'Well, he can't spell hypnotist, so he thought hippo was the closest.'

'And what has all this - very interesting though it may be - got to do with the dweeb ... sorry, husband ... and me?' I shoot the question at the local plod.

'Well, that's where there might have been a problem, ma'am. Harry The Hippo's main strength is to trick people into believing they are Humphrey Bogart playing the private eye Sam Spade in The Maltese Falcon. Have you ever seen it? What a wonderful movie. ma'am. I've seen - '

'Okay, Barry Norman, enough of the film crit. What's all this about Humphrey Bogart, Sam Spade and The Maltese Falcon?'

'Well, Harry The Hippo came round to the station an hour or so ago to tell me he had put your husband under his spell. It only works on the really feeble-minded, apparently, but it seemed to work a treat with you husband. Started talking like Bogart right away. Incredible. Bought the whole package.'

'And?'

'Well, Harry The Hippo has just told us he forgot to take your husband out of the trance. I bet your other half believes he is still Bogart. Have you noticed any changes in him recently?'

'One or two.'

'Well, there you go. He probably still thinks he's Bogie.'

'And how do we get Bogie back to being a doofus?' I ask immediately.

'Harry The Hippo says it's simple. Just snap your fingers and say: "Falcon." As simple as that.'

'As simple as that?' I ask

'Yes, ma'am, do that and your husband will be returned as good as new. He won't remember a thing.'

I close the door in PC McIvor's face.

I go to the front room. Bogart is now relaxed as he sips his bourbon on the rocks in a tall glass. 'Well handled, sister,' he smirks. 'You did okay, for a dumb Doris.'

I snap my fingers and shout: 'Falcon!' There's a moment's silence. Then, the pillock spits out his mouthful of bourbon all over the carpet and smiles broadly at me. 'Hello, my vision of all that is lovely in the paradise of loveliness,' he squeaks.

'I could do with a couple of ice buckets and a couple of bottles of Prosecco to keep the ice company,' I order, just to make sure. 'Pronto!'

'I will take care of that this minute, my beautiful of all beauties. Would you like three bottles? Maybe four? I know you have been working so hard recently and I think you deserve a little time off. I'll get the drinks and then I will paint the spare bedroom. Okay? And then I'll wash your car,' he trills happily as he flounces off in the direction of the kitchen while throwing the fedora and trench coat in the corner.

It won't be long before I am administering dull ones once more, dear friends.

All is once more right in the world. I think I'll get on the outside of a few bottles of Prosecco to celebrate.

LOCKDOWN, day 202

Saturday, October 10

Today, I awake with a cunning little plan that should make the morning extremely interesting. Unfortunately for the dweeb, he is going to play a major role in my entertainment.

So, with a bit of spring in my step, I launch myself out of the pit, making sure I do not tread on the little dork's discarded Edward G Robinson pyjamas (don't ask) and I head across the bedroom for a thorough and damn good rummage (oh, for goodness sake, you lot at the back, keep it down, please).

I fumble with a mass of clothing in an effort to find something suitable for another day in hell that may be brightened by the antics of the village idiot. Finally, I select my favourite Peter Cushing jumpsuit (don't ask) and I make my way to the fridge for some added inspiration aka Prosecco.

Before I thunder a few jolts beyond my thrapple, dear friends and fellow-sympathisers, I want to let you know that what is about to unfold is not done through malice. No, not at all. I see it as a little bit of payback on the miniscule halfwit who shares the marital bed.

What has brought about this turn of events? I hear you ask.

I am loathe to admit this, but I thought the dingbat looked quite alluring last night. Yes, dear friends, you are quite correct, vast quantities of bubbles had sailed their way to Happy Valley at this point. Normally, of course, he has the sex appeal of something messy and sticky you have trod on in the street. Last night, though, I imagined him as a cross between Cary Grant and Bruce Forsyth. As I say, I was quite drunk.

'Anyway, nutter,' I said, 'how about you and I get a little frisky?'

'What do you mean, my angel, my reason for living?' he squeaked.

'A little frisky,' I repeated. 'Don't you remember a little frisky?'

To be fair, it had been awhile since I had any amorous feelings for the waste of skin.

'A little frisky?' he asked again.

'Yes, a little frisky,' I returned, this time quite a bit louder.

'Can you give me a clue, my sweet coconut?' he pleaded.

'You and I can go upstairs, 'I urged, 'and get a little frisky.'

I could see the penny had dropped.

'I see,' he whimpered, 'and you want me to do both?'

Naturally, I administered a dull one at that precise point and went to my scratcher on my own, leaving the drongo in a shapeless heap on the floor.

I ask you, what's a gal to do? So, I feel some retribution coming the way of the buffoon. After getting on the outside of some much-needed suds, I repair to the front room where the pitiful wretch is still lying prone on the floor. I wonder for a split-second if I have administered a dull one too many.

I kick him in the ribs to make sure he is still breathing. (This is not something I recommend to would-be medical practitioners, by the way.)

He grunts and wheezes. Unluckily, for me and the rest of the universe, the dumbbell will live to fight another day.

Of course, I rush to his aid, picking him up one-handed by the neck and throwing him on the sofa. 'You must have had a terrible dream,' I say as I give him a slap across the face to make sure he responds.

'Yes, that must have been it, my awesomeness,' he squeals. 'Just another bad dream. I've had quite a lot of those in the past year or so, haven't I?'

I don't answer because I believe it is a rhetorical question.

'Let me wrap up your wounds,' I say as I head for the well-used medical cabinet in the bathroom. I stop by the kitchen to drain another bottle of bubbles.

Fortified, I pick up enough bandages to swathe a Pharaoh's mummy - and daddy, too, when I think about it - and start to wind them round his empty cranium. I cover his face, remembering to leave holes for his little beady eyes. I don't bother, however, about the mouth; he's never had anything interesting to say, anyway, as you must know by now, dear friends.

I can see he is still groggy. I lift him by one of his protruding ears that managed to escape the bandaging.

I go to the front window to check out the vile Mrs Bottomley-Smythe, owner of the local tearoom and the OAP vigilante situation. I smile.

I drag the protesting pillock to the front door and throw him out into the street.

'He's all yours, girls,' I cry to the unruly mob stationed at the tearoom HQ.

You should have seen him move, dear friends. He got up from his prone position and raced head-first into a lamppost. He reeled back from that, saw the converging mass of screaming and wailing harridans, tried to find his bearings and took off down the road as fast as his diminutive legs would carry him, with Mrs Wilberforce, purple bloomers at her ankles, leading the chase.

You could hear his muffled shrieks for miles.

I go to the fridge to pour a pint of Prosecco and quaff it in just about one go.

What is it they say, dear friends? Revenge is a dish best served cold? I pour another to the brim.

LOCKDOWN, day 207

Thursday, October 15

Today, I awake, dear friends and fellow-sympathisers, which seems like an awfully good idea. Now for the rest of the day in hell.

After I have taken a minute or two to unglue my peepers, I swing my legs out of the pit and neatly sidestep his discarded Nelly the Elephant pyjamas (don't ask).

As you are all aware by now, I do enjoy a good fumble in the morning (Edina! So early?) in my crowded wardrobe for what will be my ensemble of the day. Luckily, I locate my favourite Spike Mulligan jumpsuit (don't ask).

There are no noises from the front room this morning. Last time that happened, the pillock was doing a muted Ringo Starr impersonation, playing a set of air-drums with a pair of very real drumsticks. I'm confident that isn't the case today, however: somehow, those drumsticks got shoved where the sun doesn't shine, and the husband hasn't been able to walk right since.

Anyway, in time-honoured fashion, I head straight to the fridge for breakfast and I immediately get on the outside of a bottle of bubbles. Refreshed - and dare I say it, fortified? (oh, for goodness sake, you lot at the back) - I am ready for a second go at the suds. Thankfully, the Prosecco doesn't put up too much of a struggle and the second soldier goes quietly to Happy Valley.

Now I feel as though I can face whatever awaits me. I hold my breath and push open the door to be confronted with the deranged one standing in what looks like a makeshift boxing ring. If I am not mistaken, he also appears to be wearing a pair of Mrs Wilberforce's purple bloomers. I had heard the rumours about her undercrackers going missing on a regular basis from the washing line, but I dismissed that as total madness. Who in

164

their right mind would want to nick a pair of Mrs Wilberforce's outsized purple bloomers? Nevertheless, here the drongo stands, adorned in what looks uncannily like a pair of those gigantic underthings.

He is topless, unfortunately, and the purple unmentionables just about swamp his puny frame. He is wearing a pair of well-scuffed sandals and I note he has found my long-lost green mittens. I wondered where they had got to.

'I'll moider da bum,' he mumbles.

'Yes, good morning to you, too, nutter,' I say by way of a pleasant exchange.

'Da bum goes down in four,' he mutters.

'Well, my little pile of warthog droppings, what we have here is a communication problem,' I say. 'I will use English as it is meant to be spoken and is understood throughout the land, and you can speak as though you have just recovered from falling on your head from a rather large building. Okay?'

'I'll moider day bum,' he repeats.

'Yes, I think I've got that one, my little imbecilic object of ridicule,' I reply. 'Presumably, da bum goes down in four, is that correct?'

He shuffles his feet, goes into a weird sort of hunch and touches his nose a couple times. 'Da title's mine,' he squeaks.

'Are you by any chance a boxer?' I ask politely. 'And you are ready to pulverise the bottom, knock him out in the fourth round and win the title? Is that what you are telling me? Nod if you understand, you little cretin.'

He nods his empty head.

'That's fine, we are on the same page now. So, I believe boxers have to be fighting fit, quite literally, when they go into the ring. Would I be correct in that assumption? A nod of the head will suffice, halfwit.'

He nods his napper.

'In that case, may I suggest you get in training?' I say. (As you can see, dear friends, a cunning plan is beginning to hatch.) 'You have a giant rubber weeble toy, do you not, in that room at the back of the cottage? The sort that wobbles, but doesn't fall down?'

His little face lights up. He races off to the back of beyond and, lo and behold, comes back with the giant blown-up rubber image of Sid James (don't ask).

He follows me into the back garden, snorting and puffing all the way through the house, waving his mittens at the non-existent crowd as though he's entering Madison Square Garden.

I make sure the Sid Jamesweeble toy is blown up to its absolute maximum. I set it up in the middle of the garden and tell the dumbbell to practice a couple of punches. He swings and hits Sid on his already misshapen snoot. He giggles and punches it again.

I repair to the fridge for a third bottle of Prosecco and settle back to watch the work-out. It's only a matter of time, of course, before there is a mishap, dear friends.

Sure enough, around about the tenth swing of one of his scrawny arms, he trips and grabs hold of the rocking weeble toy. There is a loud bang, followed by a massive expulsion of air. The little sap holds on for dear life as the apparatus takes off at high speed over the cottage roof in the general direction of the tearoom where the obnoxious Mrs Bottomley-Smythe and her confederates are waiting, as ever.

I see the purple bloomers flutter back to earth, shaken loose during the rush of wind that has blown the village idiot in the general direction of his sworn enemy.

He'll be naked, apart from a pair of green mittens when he hits the ground. This is going to take some explaining, dear friends.

I hear shrieks, yelps and crazy banshee-like noises coming from across the road.

The drongo has landed.

Doesn't look like he'll be 'moidering any bums' today.

LOCKDOWN, day 211

Monday, October 19

Today, I awake and I am immediately aware there is a dark cloud hovering inside Chez Gerda. I don't mean literally, of course, dear friends and fellow sympathisers.

As soon as my peepers become unstuck to greet another day in hell, I am aware of an atmosphere. I do believe the dweeb is in a sulk.

After regaining consciousness, following the administration of a dull one when he lost the draw as he went for his water pistol and I was dead on the money with a particularly deft throw of the Prosecco bottle (empty, of course), the miniscule drongo who shares the marital bed went into a huff.

Now this is most unusual, I have to confess. Normally when he is knocked out for a couple of hours - the record so far is six hours of which I am inordinately proud - I tell him he had been hit by falling masonry. He awakes, I tell him not to worry about a thing, I have heroically cleaned up the debris once again and everything in the world is hunky dory. The village idiot usually takes me at my word, dear friends.

However, when he stirred and came back to the planet last night, after a disappointing one-and-a-half hours of lying prone on the carpet in his Lone Ranger outfit, he seemed to have a perfect recollection of the incident.

'Why did you strike me, oh sweetness and light?' he asked, his lower lip trembling. 'I was having so much fun.'

'You were wrecking the house, you little nutter."

'I was just playing horsey,' he whimpered.

'You were turning the front room into a war zone, you deranged halfwit,' I chided as gently as I could.

167

He sat in the sofa with arms folded and in an obvious huff for the rest of the evening. It would have been a little more easy to take him seriously if he had removed his giant homemade mask and oversized ten-gallon hat.

I was concerned for about a millisecond and then I decided another bottle of bubbles might ease the tension. It worked a treat, dear friends. I was as tension-free as a newt by the time I clambered up the stairs to the room of ZZZZZZS that evening. Or it could have been this morning. I'll never know.

Anyway, I awake and I am aware I may have to take the dork in hand (oh, for goodness sake, you lot at the back) and point out the error of his ways.

I slide my tootsies from the pit and neatly sidestep his discarded Captain Pugwash pyjamas (don't ask) and I head for my bulging wardrobe for a damn good rummage (Edina!) I pull out my favourite Beryl Reid jumpsuit (don't ask) and I prepare for another day at the coalface of life where every ticking minute is sixty seconds' worth of angst.

Naturally, I head for the fridge for a bottle of breakfast. It goes down rather well, maybe too well. Ho hum, another quickly follows and I then cross the hall to face the miseries of the front room.

The little drongo is sitting there, wearing his best Robin Hood outfit. I swear there will be some swift retribution if he goes anywhere near his bow and arrow which are perched up against the furniture (or what's left of it after last night's shenanigans with all that 'Hi Ho Silver ... AWAY' nonsense).

As I walk into the room, the dimwit doesn't say a word. So far so good, I think.

'Good morning, buffoon,' I say by way of a late-morning greeting.

'I was having so much fun,' he mumbles. 'You didn't have to hit me over the head with a bottle.'

'It was for your own good, my miniscule pillock,' I reply.

'Clobbering the Lone Ranger over the head with a heavy object and leaving him flattened on the floor was for my benefit?' he bleats.

'Well, of course, you little waste of oxygen,' I say. 'I have noticed you have become a little reliant on Tonto over the years. The Lone Ranger gets himself into scrapes and his loyal Native American sidekick gets him out of trouble time and time again. Understand?'

'No, I don't,' he whimpers, which doesn't surprise me. You can tell, dear friends, that the doofus needs things explained to him quite slowly.

'Do you remember the time the Lone Ranger and Tonto were riding along one day and suddenly they were surrounded by about thirty very angry Apaches?'

He shakes his nifty Robin Hood-capped cranium. (Idly, I wonder where he got the rather large and exotic feather from. There's probably a naked pheasant wondering around the neighbourhood as we speak.)

'Well, that was the day the Lone Ranger found out just how loyal Tonto really was,' I press home. 'The Apaches were circling the Lone Ranger and Tonto and he said to his Red Indian friend: "I think we're in trouble, Tonto". And Tonto said: "What's this 'we', white man?"'

After another hour or so, admittedly with the help of a bottle of Prosecco (purely for medicinal purposes, of course) I manage to win him around.

He is astonished to learn the Lone Ranger is a work of fiction. Naturally, with the brain the size of a dried-up pea, he doesn't want to believe me. But I force the issue.

His little lower lip begins to tremble again, almost uncontrollably.

'But Popeye is real, isn't he?' he asks, his little beady eyes wide open in expectation.

'Yes, of course,' I reassure him. Well, dear friends, I can't shatter all his dreams and fantasies at once.

You should see his little face. He starts to rock from side to side and croaks: 'I'm Popeye the sailor man ... .'

The pipsqueak, dressed as Robin Hood, seems quite happy as he squeaks out the little ditty.

Job done, methinks, dear friends. I eye the bow and arrow at his side and I make sure I have an empty bottle of Prosecco handy. Just in case things get a tad rowdy.

I repair to the fridge while the strains of 'I'm Popeye the sailor man' bounce around the house,

Normality has arrived. Or as near normality as you will get in Chez Gerda.

LOCKDOWN, day 218

Monday, October 26

Today, I awake with a rather large smile on my face. (Don't even go there, you lot at the back.)

I have the marital bed to myself and there is no sign of the dweeb. Just the way I like it.

When I was courting the little pipsqueak (yes, dear friends and fellow sympathisers, we did actually go through a form of courtship. Hard to believe, isn't it? Please believe me when I tell you I was not on hallucinogenic drugs back then. Those came later.) I once asked him about his previous conquests. He got a little tongue-tied, which I found kind of cute. Now, of course, it drives me bonkers.

'Did you have difficulty getting girls to share your bed?' I asked.

'I have difficulty getting girls to share the same postcode,' he replied.

I thought he was joking. Now I know better.

Anyway, I digress, dear friends. Sunshine is clattering off the bedroom windows and I believe we may be seeing a last rush of glorious rays before the grey clouds descend. I aim to make the most of this pleasant weather, so I kick off the sheets and practically bounce out of the scratcher (memo to self: get on a diet) neatly sidestepping his discarded Pepe Le Pew pyjamas (don't ask). Once again, I indulge in a right good forage (Edina! That's enough of that!) in my bulging wardrobe and extricate my favourite Dave Dee, Dozy, Beaky, Mick and Tich jumpsuit (don't ask)

Downstairs, I get on the outside of a bottle of Prosecco (today is not the day to break the habit of a lifetime, dear friends) and swiftly move onto a second helping.

Fortified - I said 'fortified', Edina - I head across the hall towards the front room and I wonder what lies behind the door. One push can often lead to a surprise and unforgettable adventure.

The dork has treated me to the Lone Ranger and Robin Hood in recent days. I wonder what is in store this sunny Monday late-morning.

Once again, I am not disappointed. Sitting on the sofa is William Tell.

'Good morning, nutter,' I say with as much warmth as I can muster.

'Ja,' he returns. I reckon that is the extent of the dingbat's German.

'So, we are dressed as a Swiss folk hero today, I see, my brain-dead spouse. Is there any reason for today's garb?'

'Ja,' he replies. As a bonus he adds: 'Apple.' He points to a crossbow, arrow and a piece of fruit resting on the sofa.

'Oh, I see, you complete waste of skin, we are going to re-enact the moment William Tell narrowly missed giving his son a middle eye while trying to slice an apple in half? Is that it?'

'Ja,' he nods his head which is encased in his great granny Bertha's best funeral hat. The Good Lord only knows where he unearthed that. It is green and has a small feather protruding from it. (Note to fashion houses: Why?)

'Are you perchance looking for a volunteer to balance an apple on their head?' I ask.

'Ja,' he trills and looks excited.

'And then you will take aim and fire an arrow at the apple? Is that right?'

'Ja,' he squeaks and once again jumps up and down on the sofa.

'Good luck with that, bampot,' I reply.

The husband/William Tell/halfwit frowns. His little shoulders slump forward and I swear I can detect a small whimper. He fumbles in his Great Auntie Elsie's brown reinforced tights for a handkerchief.

In moments like these, dear friends, I feel for the miniscule sap. He doesn't ask for much in life, so I ask him: 'Do you still have your extremely lifelike Guy Fawkes effigy?'

His little face lights up and he claps his tiny hands. 'Ja!' he exclaims.

'Why don't you fetch it, I'll set it up in the back garden and you can take a shot at it?' I say reasonably.

He leaps out of the sofa and races off to his room at the back of the cottage where not even the SAS would dream of entering.

What can go wrong, dear friends?

Inside a minute, the buffoon rushes back and holds aloft Guy Fawkes. He waves it in the air and exclaims: 'Ja ... apple.'

We repair to the back garden where I roll over a rubbish bin and sit Guy Fawkes in an upright position. I place the apple (wax, of course) on the effigy's head and everything is set for the big shoot. I check the coast is clear - I wouldn't like the villainous Mrs Bottomley-Smythe, owner of the local tearoom, or any of her crazed and blood-thirsty crones to be hit smack in the face with a sharp object. Well, now that I think about it ... No, let's have an accident-free day, keep the pilchard happy and then I can indulge in some Prosecco-guzzling for the remainder of this fine Monday. Sounds like a plan, doesn't it?

'Okay, Looney Tunes, everything is good to go. All you have to do now is point your crossbow at the apple and take aim. Okay?'

'Ja ... apple,' he says as he stands about twelve yards from the target. He lines up his shot and fires. Whooooooooooosh. The arrow flies through the air. He misses the apple by about a mile, give or take. Instead, the arrow ricochets off the side of the garage, zips across the garden, picks up a sheet that was in the drying area and takes off towards the sky. It's like watching a high-speed ghost as it flashes upwards.

Mr Davidson, our neighbour who likes to be called 'Daredevil Davidson', just happens to be sailing past as he paraglides across the tranquil blue skies above the village. Bad timing, Daredevil.

He becomes entangled with the sheet and veers off to the left on his way to making an unscheduled stop, probably in the nearby farmer's fields which are normally festooned in cow dung at this time of year. If he's lucky, he'll get a soft landing.

I tell William Tell it might be a good idea to depart the scene of the crime.

'Ja,' he says.

That's the excitement over for the day, dear friends. The pillock needs to go and lie down in a darkened room as I head for the fridge.

BREAKING NEWS: Daredevil Davidson is recovered on a hillside later on that evening. He won't be paragliding for some considerable time. He won't be walking for some considerable time, either, because broken legs sort of make that manoeuvre difficult. He'll be hospitalised for at least a month, I have been informed. Police are baffled.

Sshhhhhhhhhhhh, dear friends, I know my secret is safe with you.

LOCKDOWN, day 221

Thursday, October 29

Today, I awake and roll out of bed. That's the easy part. Now I have to get off the floor.

Yes, a few Proseccos floated beyond my necktie last night, I must confess, dear friends and fellow sympathisers.

I realise there may be a few of you out there who are a tad alarmed at my daily consumption of bubbles. Please allow me to allay those fears. I drink vast quantities of suds for fortification which I am sure you will agree is a required commodity when you share a marital bed with a dweeb.

I admit I did suffer mild bouts of depression shortly after I allowed the little drongo to take me up the aisle (oh, for goodness sake you lot at the back, not again with the sniggering).

I did go to a pharmacist one day and I asked him for some anti-depressant pills.

He informed me I required a prescription.

I showed him a photograph of the dork and explained I had just married him.

I left with a six-month supply of pills. The nice man even arranged the loan of a wheelbarrow to transport the bottles home.

However, that was a long, long time ago, I am delighted to relate. Now it's a slalom through lakes of Prosecco to keep me on an even keel. The government really should put this delightful aperitif on prescription. It may not help with depression, but you'll probably be too hungover to realise you are depressed in the first place.

I'm sorry, dear friends, I digress. Where was I? Oh, yes, on my knees as I crawl past his discarded Richard Nixon pyjamas (don't ask) and get unsteadily back to my feet. I lurch towards my exploding wardrobe and

I take pot luck as I thrust my hand through the throng. I haul out my favourite Donald Pleasance jumpsuit (don't ask) and I head downstairs to the fridge. The bubbles have been singing my name since my peepers became unglued. It is funny how they seem to know when I most require their services.

The first bottle is a mere memory after fifty-five seconds (rather slow for me). I take the time to slosh the contents of the second bottle into my trusty pint pot and those suds are devoured, too, in double-quick time.

I manage to straighten up. Have you seen those images of the ascent of man? You know the ones where he goes from a chimpanzee through the ape, gorilla and cave-dweller stages until he becomes a human being? Well, I cut the time down to a couple of minutes while it took that gink centuries. Girl power!

All is silent in the front room. What is the miniscule pillock up to today, I wonder? I push open the door and am confronted by Superman. Well, not quite Clark Kent's alter ego, but some scrawny little creature wearing a baggy blue jumpsuit with a handwritten 'S' on his puny chest.

He has completed the superhero look with a pair of enormous crimson undercrackers which, sadly, he doesn't quite fill in the manner of Christopher Reeve, and, naturally, he has discovered his massive red wellies that could double as clown's shoes. I note he has somehow got his hands on my old red velvet curtains and is utilising them as a cape.

I doubt if this particular version of Superman could save five pence never mind the world. Kryptonite? Claude's last 'gift' to the litter tray would have him keeling over backwards if it came within half-a-mile of him.

'Good morning, nutter,' I say, and I admit the words may lack a smidgen of warmth.

'Good morning, Lois,' he squeaks.

'My name is Gerda, you feeble-minded oaf,' I reply.

'You are Lois Lane,' he whimpers, 'and you are my girlfriend at the Daily Planet.'

'Girlfriend?' I retort. 'You couldn't get a nod from a rocking horse, you little creep.' I think he has caught me on a bad day. Please forgive me, dear friends, for being a little curt today, I'm not really in the mood for his shenanigans.

I haven't administered a dull one for a few days, but that streak may be broken this morning.

'The Joker is in town and he is threatening mayhem,' mumbles SuperSap.

'Oh, dear, The Joker!' I feign horror. 'Is he going to tell some of his best rib-ticklers? How cruel can he be? Who could forget this classic? "I had the ploughman's lunch the other day. He wasn't half mad."'

The husband/Superman/buffoon says nothing.

'Or how about: "My dog took a bite out of my leg the other day and a friend said: 'Did you put anything on it?' I said: "No, he liked it as it was".'

The dweeb is struck dumb.

'It's strange, isn't it? You stand in the middle of a library and go "Aaaaaaaaaagh!" and everyone just stares at you. But you do that on an airplane and everyone joins in.'

Silence.

'I was going to see the doctor, but I changed my mind. He's not a very good doctor. All his patients are sick.'

More silence.

'All day yesterday I heard ringing in my ears. Then I picked up the phone and it stopped.'

'Please, please, no more,' pleads the Man of Steel/Candyfloss. Everyone's a critic, dear friends.

'Okay,' I concede, 'let's go outside and you can show me some of your superpowers.' Naturally, I have hatched a cunning plan. I tell Superman to stand on top of the log store and he dutifully scrambles onto its roof. Nothing to worry about, it's only about five feet off the ground.

We had an 'It's a Knock-out' competition at our last village gala day and I managed to purloin (ahem) a few of the giant rubber bouncy balls. I knew they would come in handy someday. Today is that day. I roll them down from the garage and make sure they are pumped up to the maximum. Satisfied, I set up six of them in front of the log store.

'All set, Mr Superman,' I say. 'Impress me with your super powers.'

I stand back and yell: 'Look up to the sky! Is it a bird? Is it a plane? It's Superman!'

This galvanises the little dumbbell. I swear I can see his pygmy-like chest swell to the size of a walnut. He prepares for take-off.

'Faster than a speeding - ' and then he leaps onto the bouncy balls.

BDOOOOOOOOOOOIIIIIIIIIIIIING!

' - bullet.' He takes off at an alarming rate, his crimson undercrackers being left behind as he zips off into the wild blue yonder, velvet curtains flapping furiously behind him. He clears the garage with plenty to spare.

I repair to the kitchen. The dingbat will no doubt be found head-first in a pile of cowpats someone in the nearby farmer's land. Hopefully, Farmer McTavish will hose down Superman before returning him to Krypton.

By which time, courtesy of an ocean of suds, I will very possibly be on a planet of my own. Happy days, dear friends.

If you see something flying through the air in your neighbourhood, it probably won't be a bird or a plane. It's more likely to be SuperDweeb. Give him a wave for me, will you?

LOCKDOWN, day 224

Sunday, November 1

Today, I awake to a rather strange request from the dweeb who shares the marital bed. No, you lot at the back, not THAT sort of strange request. (More's the pity.)

My peepers are just becoming unglued to greet another day in hell when I am aware of some strange yodelling or hollering from the front room. I think possibly the little drongo is in pain. Maybe the ceiling has collapsed on top of him or something trivial like that.

I aim to put the investigation into the racket on top that late-morning's to-do list as soon as I am fortified with a few jolts of much-required Prosecco. As I make my way downstairs for my bottled breakfast there are still some strange shrills coming from the front room. Maybe a bookcase has toppled over and pinned the halfwit to the floor?

First things first, dear friends and fellow-sympathisers. I swing open the door to bubble paradise and yank out a bottle. Sixty seconds later and I'm onto the second.

I cross towards the front room where the strange screeching noises are still emitting from. Maybe he is strangling Claude the cat? I have warned Claude about weeing in his hair when he is asleep or, more likely, unconscious.

I open the door to be greeted by the dork dressed in a rather large and ill-fitting white suit which has musical symbols dotted all over it. All those semi-quavers make me feel a tad thirsty and I think for a moment about a second visit to the fridge. I decide to learn more.

He is wearing a red shirt with frills down the front, the sort Carmen Miranda used to wear back in the days when she used to shake her maracas (oh for goodness sake, Edina! Show a little decorum, please).

The scuffed brown sandals complete the look. I realise the weird sounds I have been hearing are the miniscule jerk's efforts at singing. He is holding a hairbrush in his right hand and moving like someone who has just trod on a live electric cable.

'Good morning, nutter,' I say by way of a greeting.

He stops screaming and it is that moment he makes his bizarre request.

I am fairly affronted, dear friends. My immediate thought, of course, is to administer a dull one.

I thought he said: 'Let's have a kiss, my little strawberry tart.'

Well, I wasn't having any of that nonsense, I can tell you. Then he repeats his line.

'Let's have a quiz, my little strawberry tart,' he says.

My goodness, was I relieved or was I relieved?

'Can we have a pop quiz, please, oh, most magnificent vision of beauty?' he asks.

I think about it for a moment, dear friends. I am aware this is lockdown day 224 (count 'em and weep) and we are now going into the eighth month of this infernal intrusion into our lives. I decide to give him a break and, no, I don't mean his scrawny neck.

I relent and accept his request. Actually, this can work in my favour. The dingbat doesn't really know too much about pop music. Let's face it, the little twerp doesn't know too much about anything.

His all-time favourite album is Mantovani plays Peter, Paul and Mary with Keith Moon guesting on drums, Live at the Hippodrome, Great Cleethorpes circa 1964. It's a bit of a collector's item. It lasts exactly two minutes and twelve seconds before Moon, who would go on to become 'The Wild Man of the The Who', kicks over his drum kit, throws a cymbal at Mantovani, attacks the solo triangle player and sets fire to the wind section. .

Sorry, dear friends, I digress. My apologies. Let's get straight to the quiz. First, though, I repair to the fridge to select three soldiers, place them in the ice buckets, and cart them through to the front room. This could be a long day.

'Okay, you miniscule waste of oxygen, here are the rules,' I say as I take my seat opposite the buffoon who has commandeered the sofa.

'For every question you get wrong, I am allowed a swig of Prosecco. Okay?'

He nods his vacuumed cranium.

'Right to start us off, here is an easy one. When Ringo Starr was growing up in Liverpool, he had a pet goldfish. Can you tell me the goldfish's name? You have a minute to respond, starting now.'

The befuddled one looks a tad perplexed before taking a guess. 'Albert,' he offers.

'No, sorry, that is the wrong answer,' I say as I lift a bottle of Prosecco to my welcoming lips and guzzle for a few seconds. 'That was, in fact, a trick question. Ringo Starr never had a pet gold fish growing up in Liverpool.'

You should have seen his little face, dear friends. I thought he was going to burst into tears. His lower lip was trembling in overdrive.

'Okay, second question, and I wish you better luck with this one. Here we go. Dave Clark, drummer and leader of the Dave Clark Five, had a favourite hairspray. Can you name it?'

The twerp looks thunderstruck.

'Would you care to take a guess?' I ask.

'Albert,' he trills.

'Sorry, you're wrong again.' Once more I reach for the bottle in the ice bucket and take a glug. It was "Dave Clark's Hairspray For Men". You were close with Albert, though. Now, this is the third and final question in today's pop quiz. If you get this one wrong, I get to partake in Prosecco all day while you do the housework, complete the washing, redecorate the bathroom and cut the grass in both the front and back gardens. Okay?'

The simpleton nods his head. 'I'm ready,' he squeaks.

'Alvin Stardust's real name was not Alvin Stardust. Was it A: Bjorn Borg; B: Sir Alf Ramsey or C: Tammy Wynette? The clock starts ticking now.'

The dumbbell stares straight ahead. I know this is a sure fire sign he is trying to concentrate. 'Was it Bjorn Borg?' he asks.

'Is that your final answer,' I say, as the drama mounts.

He nods his empty head.

'Sorry, it was, in fact, Bernard William Jewry. He was also known in the sixties as Shane Fenton before settling for the rather absurd Alvin Stardust.'

'But you said - '

'Yes, I do believe I offered you the choice of three, didn't I? Bjorn Borg, Sir Alf Ramsey or Tammy Wynette, a rather good selection, I must say. I never said Alvin Stardust's true identity was among that trio of rather hip funsters. You should have been paying attention, my little insignificant other.'

I start on a fresh bottle of Prosecco. 'I would begin with the front garden, if I were you. It might rain later today.'

Head down, the little saddo climbs off the sofa and I can see his shoulders heaving.

'And do a good job,' I bark. 'I will be inspecting it later.'

Harsh? You bet, dear friends. I'm going into the eighth month of lockdown much in the manner as I did the first seven and this is the way I intend to continue. I almost feel sorry for the dweeb.

I said almost.

LOCKDOWN, day 250

Wednesday, November 25

Today, I awake and I realise I have some bad news for the dweeb. It will be my solemn duty to inform the person who shares the marital bed that Christmas has been cancelled. The government had already decreed there will be no fun and games to complete a dreadful year. Now it's official.

He really does welcome the Festive season and I realise how much he enjoys pulling his cracker (oh, for goodness sake you lot at the back, a modicum of decorum, if you please).

Normally, I sit the little drongo in front of the TV and he laughs all the way through the Morecambe and Wise Christmas Specials - including the adverts. As you all know by now, dear friends and fellow sympathisers, he does get a tad confused.

I recall a few years ago while I was stuffing the turkey (Edina! Enough of that, if you don't mind) and I heard some strange noises emitting from the front room. Naturally, I believed it was last night's Brussel sprouts repeating on the dork, but, after about ten minutes, I decided to investigate.

The little blighter had dressed up as Santa Claus and in his excitement as Eric belted out: 'Give me sunshine' had begun munching on the white beard. When I finally raced through - well, trundled, actually - to the front room he was coughing, spluttering and his face was turning blue. I could see a mouthful of Father Christmas' beard just about to disappear down his thrapple.

Of course, I administered a dull one with an empty bottle of Prosecco that somehow just happened to be in my hand.

Wham! And down went Santa, thumping his head off the fireplace as he toppled.

While the halfwit was out for the count, I managed to pry his jaws open and pull about ten inches of fake beard from his throat. (No applause required, dear friends, I was just doing what any gal would do.)

When the buffoon regained consciousness about half-an-hour later, I had a stern word with him.

'What on earth were you thinking, you little pillock?,' I asked with a fair bit of understanding given the circumstances. 'You could have choked to death and I don't know where your insurance policies are. How selfish can you get? Leaving me a widow on Christmas Day and with a full turkey untouched.'

Have you ever seen Santa Claus grovel? It was a pitiful sight, dear friends.

After he had spent about an hour or so thanking me for saving his worthless life, I had to ask him the question again.

'What on earth were you thinking, you little pillock?' I repeated.

'You know I get a bit muddled ...'

'Doolally would be a better word.'

' ... well, I thought it was candy floss.' He smiled his annoying little pathetic smile. 'It was quite nice, actually.'

So, dear friends, that is what I will have to contend with this late morning as I swing my tooties out of the scratcher and neatly sidestep his Quasimodo pyjamas (don't ask). I heave and haul through the mountain of cardis in my wardrobe until I get my hands on something and I wrench it from the pile. I am happy with today's garb, my favourite Acker Bilk jumpsuit (don't ask) and I head downstairs where my first port of call will be - you've guessed - the fridge.

I need a right good fortification - Edina! Final warning! - before I break the news to the diminutive pest who has been so looking forward to dressing up as an elf this year. Not that he would need to do much dressing up to pass for an elf, when I think about it. He is about two-thirds of the way there already with his stunted growth, puny frame and glaikit look.

I get on the outside of a couple of bottles of Prosecco and am now ready for a fresh day in hell with the dullard.

I push open the front door and he is sitting quietly reading the latest copy of 'Knitting For Grannies'. He likes looking at balls of wool for reasons known only to himself. Not unusual when you have the brain power akin to something Claude regularly deposits in her litter tray. The magazine is upside down.

'Hello, nutter,' I say by way of expressing my joy at seeing the pilchard.

Before he says anything - I can see he is concentrating on a particularly fetching yarn of blue wool - I add: 'Christmas is off.'

That gets his attention. Pronto. 'Wh-a-a-a-t?' he mutters.

'Santa's dead,' I decide to break it to him gently.

'How?' he practically shrieks.

'He fed a few particularly bad, off-colour carrots to Prancer, Dancer, Donner and Blitzen.'

'And?' he asks, wide-eyed, lower lip trembling.

'Well, they were flying over Finland on a practice run for the big day.'

'And?' he says, tears beginning to form at the corners of his beady little eyes.

'Blew him right out of his seat. Not so much as a ho-ho-ho as he took off somewhere over Helsinki. They're still searching for the remains.'

'Santa's dead?'

'You catch on quick, don't you?' I say with some measured sarcasm.

The poor little sucker looks as though he has been hit by a thunderbolt. He collapses on the sofa.

'But we will still have a Christmas tree, won't we?' he responds.

'Yes, of course,' I relent. 'I don't see why we can't have a Christmas tree.'

'And I can be a fairy and sit on top of it?'

I don't want to remind him that we have spent the last ten Boxing Days at the local A&E where they have had to surgically remove a fair amount of Norwegian Spruce from a place where you really shouldn't find a fair amount of Norwegian Spruce.

Well, that's something for me to look forward to, then, dear friends.

ACKNOWLEDGEMENTS

My gracious thanks to Sandy Jamieson, the Chief Executive of Ringwood Publishers, for his belief in the lockdown diaries.

A round of applause is also due to all the many staff at Ringwood who have helped make this book a reality. In particular, massive thanks are due to Daly Naughton, my Editor, for making logical sense of chaos; Boony Boon and Rowan Groat for their sterling efforts in social media promotion. Also, I doff my cap in the direction of Dave Webster for his commitment, tolerance and patience in copyediting the disparate parts into the final printed version.

A huge thanks must also go to the Ringwood Designer, Nicola Campbell, for producing the final cover and for going far beyond the call of duty to create so many very relevant illustrations that greatly enhance the visual impact of the book.

And how can I forget this little lot who have been with me every step of the way? Thank you for your support, dear friends and fellow-sympathisers:

Nicky Alexander, Janet Akhurst, Les Anderson, Susan Andrew, Carrie Ann, Dave Ansell, Julie Aris, Hellen Bach, HB Berlow, Nova Blackstock, Christine Barry Howshall, Gill Batchelor, Tina Bailey, Marian Begg, Penny Boland, Jan Booth, Barbara Boswell, Karen Boucher, Richard Boulter, Angus and Veronica Boyd, Paul Carr-Griffin, Pamela Carter, Bill Caven, Michele Charles, Wilma Chestnut, Liz Christie, Ann Clark, Anne Clarke, Sally and John Claxton, Edina Cloud, Paul Currie, Sue Clark, Marian Dawtrey, Janet Daly, Larry Diamond, Lisa Diplock, Alison Donnachie, Stella Dorey, Shirley Dudley, Elizabeth Dundas, Buster Dunne, Jeanette Dyer, Elaine Eales, Nichola Favell, John and Michelle Fox, Barbara Gail, Eileen Gallacher, Clifton Gare-Mogg, Margaret Geaney, Mary Gemmell, Kirsten and Steve Gill, Randi Gilliland, Sandra Good, June Graham, Tracey Graham, Sue Green-Steele, Jo Greenall, Margaret Hughes, Judith Harper, Julie Hall, Ursula Haines, Anne Hall, Susan Harding, Kim Hodgett, Siobhan Hogan Hamid, Kaye Howells,

Margaret Hunt, Margaret Hunter, Janice Hamilton, Susan Ingram, Fiona Jardine, Karen James. Lyndsay Jones, Anne Jones, Jan Jones, Tina Keeling, Jacqueline Kerr, Hazel Love, Louise Lucas-Saunders, Angie MacDonagh, Susan MacDemitria, Norman MacIntosh, Sue Madden, Jeff Martin, Jill Mason, Donald and Liz Mcfadyen, James McIernon, Sue McKee, Lisa Mcloughlin, Mary Mcphee, Arlene Mills, Brenda Mills, David Mills, Sian Moore, Carole Moorhouse, Mandy Morley, Sue Morrison, Elaine Mutum, Ann Myers-Brotherston, Viv and Malcolm O'Connor, Betty Perrers, Janis Packman, Isobel Rutter, Isabell Reid, Lisa Richards-Burnett, Helen Riley, Deborah and Geoff Roberts, Sandra Rudolph, Sally Rumsey, Eunice Roberts, Anna Smith, Alistair Stars, Andrea Shepherd, Mandy and Dave Shurety, Christine Skelton, Eileen Smith, Richard and Carol Smith, Maureen Sullivan, Steph Taylor, Tracey Thomas, Susan Thompson, Barbara Walsh, Iris Warr, and Doug Webb

My profuse apologies if I have overlooked anyone.

ABOUT THE AUTHOR

Gerda Gordon is a former Deputy Systems Editor of the Daily Record and Sunday Mail, two of Scotland's national newspapers.

Gerda had no thoughts or ambitions of putting a book together and, as the title suggests, it came to life during lockdown. At the beginning of the public restrictions, Gerda posted one tale on her Facebook page which she hoped would raise a smile among some of the readers. It took off from there in fairly spectacular fashion to the extent she was compelled to deliver amusing tales every day about a fictional side of life with her blundering husband aka the dweeb and her quirky neighbours in a small village.